Changing Roles of Financial Management:
Integrating Strategy, Control, and Accountability

Stephen F. Jablonsky
*The Pennsylvania State University
and The Management Communications Group*

Patrick J. Keating
San Jose State University

A publication of Financial Executives Research Foundation, Inc.

Financial Executives Research Foundation, Inc.
10 Madison Avenue
P.O. Box 1938
Morristown, New Jersey 07962-1938
(973) 898-4608

International Standard Book Number 1-885065-09-4
Library of Congress Catalog Card Number 97-60750
Printed in the United States of America

First Printing

Financial Executives Research Foundation, Inc. (FERF™) is the research affiliate of Financial Executives Institute. The basic purpose of the Foundation is to sponsor research and publish informative material in the field of business management, with particular emphasis on the practice of financial management and its evolving role in the management of business.

The views set forth in this publication are those of the authors and do not necessarily represent those of the FERF Board as a whole, individual trustees, or the members of the Advisory Committee.

FERF publications can be ordered by calling 1-800-680-FERF (U.S. and Canada only; international orders, please call 770-751-1986). Quantity discounts are available.

Advisory Committee

William P. O'Halloran (Chairman)
Senior Vice President & Controller
SunTrust Banks, Inc.

Ronald M. Dykes
Executive Vice President and CFO
BellSouth Corporation

Lou Jones
Cost Management and Business Services
   Manager (retired)
Caterpillar Inc.

J. James Lewis
Executive Vice President
Financial Executives Research Foundation, Inc.

Curt C. Nohavec
Assistant Controller—Operations Planning
The Boeing Company

William M. Sinnett
Project Manager
Financial Executives Research Foundation, Inc.

Janet F. Hastie
Director of Communications
Financial Executives Research Foundation, Inc.

Contents

Introduction

Changing Roles of Financial Management

In our initial research,[1] we looked at the ways in which financial work was changing in American corporations. We wanted to find out how financial work was being influenced by the pressures of global competition, government regulation, and technological change.

A major outcome of that research was the development of a conceptual model that could be used to describe and explain the nature of financial work at the six firms included in the original study.[2] In describing our findings to executives at other firms and to managers attending executive education programs, we found that the conceptual framework could be applied to a wide variety of firms, irrespective of industry, country, or culture. The financial organization at any firm could be described in terms of three orientations to financial work: command and control, conformance, and competitive team.

Command-and-Control Orientation
This orientation to financial work stresses the vertical flow of financial information up and down the corporate hierarchy. The financial organization serves top management by providing an independent review, evaluation, and commentary on the operating and capital investment plans of the business units.

Conformance Orientation
This orientation to financial work stresses the external flow of information prepared in accordance with reporting requirements specified by outside agencies. The financial organization serves regulators, analysts, and other external parties by complying with the rules and regulations established for demonstrating external accountability.

Competitive-Team Orientation
This orientation to financial work stresses the horizontal flow of information among all managers within the firm. The financial organization serves the business units by providing financial leadership and support services aimed at achieving the firm's strategic business objectives.

In our initial research study, we indicated that each of the firms appeared to be moving away from the command-and-control and conformance orientations and toward the competitive-team orientation.

In follow-up discussions with executives and managers (especially nonfinancial managers) at other firms, we found that the movement toward the competitive-team orientation definitely could not be generalized across other firms. Many of these managers indicated that the command-and-control and conformance orientations were alive and well within their firms. This feedback led us to wonder if a "rhetoric/reality" gap might exist between the perceptions of financial managers and nonfinancial managers.

It is one thing for financial managers to report that they embody the competitive-team orientation to financial work. It was quite another for the nonfinancial managers in their firms, the "customers" of the financial organization, to say the same thing. Based on the reactions of nonfinancial managers to the original study, it appeared that we might have been overly optimistic about a general trend toward the competitive-team orientation.

Business Advocates or Corporate Policemen?

In our second (and ongoing) research study, we developed a diagnostic questionnaire to determine the extent to which a firm's financial organization emphasized the command-and-control, conformance, or competitive-team orientation to financial work.[3] Since that study was published in 1993, the diagnostic questionnaire (DQ5) has been refined and administered to an additional 2,400 managers.[4]

In addition to the three orientations to financial work, we found that firms tend to employ one of two very different models of financial management. In some firms, financial people are considered corporate policemen. In other firms, financial people are business advocates. As we shall see, the differences are quite striking.

The Corporate Policeman Model

This model of financial management represents a combination of command-and-control and conformance orientations to financial work.

In a Corporate Policeman environment, financial people are expected to

- ☐ enforce compliance with policies and procedures,
- ☐ think in terms of oversight and surveillance,
- ☐ administer rules and regulations,
- ☐ limit access to information on a "need-to-know" basis, and
- ☐ monitor the collection and disclosure of information.

The Business Advocate Model

This model of financial management represents a combination of command-and-control and competitive-team orientations to financial work.

In a Business Advocate environment, financial people are expected to

- ☐ integrate business operations throughout the firm,
- ☐ think in terms of service and involvement,
- ☐ have a working knowledge of the business,
- ☐ encourage wide use of financial information, and
- ☐ provide financial discipline for the business operations.

As we can see from these descriptions of the Corporate Policeman and Business Advocate models, the command-and-control orientation (which is present to a greater or lesser degree in any organization) can be combined with the conformance and competitive-team orientations to create two very different models of financial management.

Figure 1 shows how we visualize the two models of financial management and three orientations to financial work fitting into a single conceptual framework.

Managers in our public and firm-specific executive education programs have no trouble identifying the location of their financial organizations on Figure 1. Typical comments we hear include the following:

> That's us. Our financial people are pure policemen with most of the emphasis on conformance for good measure.

> If you asked me last year, I would have said that our financial people were Corporate Policemen, but we just hired a new CFO, and things are beginning to change.

FIGURE 1   Changing Roles of Financial Management: Models of Financial Management

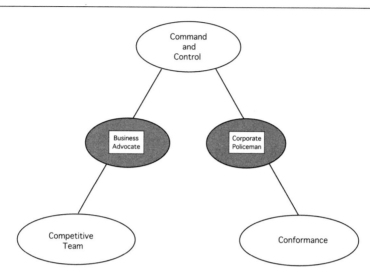

At the business-unit level, the financial people are advocates, but as you go up the hierarchy they turn into cops.

Our financial people serve as ambassadors to the corporate court. They are the only ones who know how to speak the language of corporate finance. In our firm, it's a necessary cost of doing business.

I gave our financial people high competitive teams scores. Our company is still way behind when it comes to having state-of-the-art management systems, but our financial people do the best they can with what they have to work with.

Believe it or not, our financial people are way ahead of the curve. Have you ever heard of an organization where people are fighting to get into Corporate Accounting? We could not survive without the active support of our financial people.

As these comments suggest, firms range all over the map. In executive education settings, we frequently have managers from advocate and policeman environments in the same group. In these situations, it is quite interesting to watch the reactions on the faces of the managers from policeman environments as they listen to managers from advocate

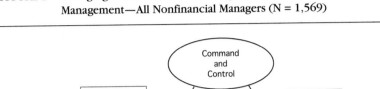

FIGURE 2   Changing Roles of Financial Management: Models of Financial Management—All Nonfinancial Managers (N = 1,569)

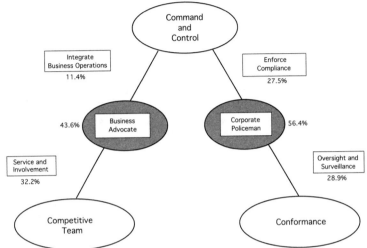

environments describe the positive role that financial people play in their firms.

Based on the responses of the 1,569 nonfinancial managers who have completed the latest version of the diagnostic questionnaire, we can add some factual "flesh" to the "bones" of our conceptual framework. Figure 2 presents the distribution of questionnaire responses we use to help managers think about the strengths and weaknesses of their own financial organizations. As we can see, the Business Advocate and Corporate Policeman models may be split into two additional submodels.[5] The Business Advocate model may be subdivided into a service-and-involvement component and an integrate-business-operations component. The Corporate Policeman model may be subdivided into an enforce-compliance component and an oversight-and-surveillance component.

Figure 2 illustrates that 32.2 percent of the nonfinancial managers surveyed believe their financial people are service oriented and get involved in the business. Another 11.4 percent view their financial people as responsible for integrating business operations throughout the firm.

The policeman side of Figure 2 shows that 28.9 percent of the nonfinancial managers surveyed believe their financial people are in place for

FIGURE 3   Business Advocates (BA) and Corporate Policemen (CP): Competing Values

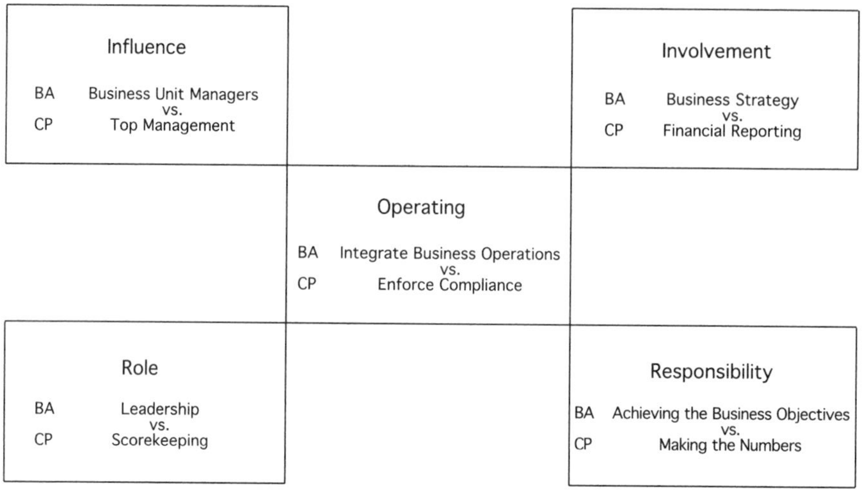

Influence		Involvement
BA Business Unit Managers vs. CP Top Management		BA Business Strategy vs. CP Financial Reporting
	Operating BA Integrate Business Operations vs. CP Enforce Compliance	
Role BA Leadership vs. CP Scorekeeping		Responsibility BA Achieving the Business Objectives vs. CP Making the Numbers

oversight and surveillance purposes. Another 27.5 percent think financial people exist to enforce compliance with the firm's policies and procedures.

Core Values and Competing Values

In a more detailed analysis of the responses to the diagnostic questionnaire, we identified a number of core values that nonfinancial managers attribute to the financial managers in their firms. As shown in Figure 3, the core values identified with the Business Advocate model of financial managers stand in stark contrast to the core values identified with the Corporate Policeman model. The core values identified with each model of financial management become *competing* values when compared with each other.[6]

If we look at the core values underlying the management operating philosophy at the center of Figure 3, we can see that financial people working in a Business Advocate environment are "integrators." They integrate the business operations throughout the firm via the financial system. Financial people working in a Corporate Policeman environment are "enforcers." They enforce compliance with policies and procedures. For this research project, we wanted to take a closer look at firms that considered their financial people more as integrators than enforcers or as moving away from being enforcers to becoming integrators.

If we look to the four corners surrounding the operating philosophy core values, we see the key words "influence," "involvement," "role," and "responsibility." Each key word can be put in the form of a question to determine the extent to which a firm's model of financial management fits the Business Advocate or Corporate Policeman profile:

1. Whom do financial people try to *influence* within the firm?

2. How do they get *involved* in the business?

3. What *roles* are they expected to play within the firm?

4. What are their major *responsibilities* within the firm?

Influence

As we can see from Figure 3, Business Advocates try to influence or serve the business-unit managers. Corporate Policemen try to influence or serve top management. In the case of Business Advocates, financial people are considered to be members of the business unit teams. In the case of Corporate Policemen, financial people are considered to be advisors to line management and are not involved in the business.

Involvement

Business Advocates are involved in the firm's overall business strategy. They share an understanding of the business with their operating manager counterparts and focus on achieving the financial targets included in the business units' strategic plan. Corporate Policemen limit their involvement to reviewing operating expenditures and preparing the monthly, quarterly, and annual reports.

Role

Business Advocates play a leadership role in the business operations. In their role as members of the business unit team, they provide business leadership and financial support services to the entire management team. Corporate Policemen play a more limited scorekeeping and recordkeeping role. In some cases, they also get involved in monitoring the operating and capital budgeting process.

Responsibility

Business Advocates are responsible for helping the team achieve its business objectives, and they do this by focusing on what needs to be done to improve the bottom line. In this environment, financial people are responsible for maintaining a cost and profitability reporting system that supports the business units. Corporate Policemen are responsible for achieving the quarterly financial numbers. Financial people hold line management accountable for the financial performance of the firm on behalf of top management. They do this through the use of a budget/variance reporting system.

The comparison of the competing values suggests that it would be almost impossible for a single financial organization to be both a Business Advocate and a Corporate Policeman at the same time.

Extending the Original *Changing Roles* Research Program

As mentioned above, we have revised and refined our diagnostic questionnaire to the point where we can help senior executives assess the extent to which their financial organization fits the Business Advocate or Corporate Policeman model. This baseline information puts these executives in a better position to develop a plan for changing their financial organization where deemed necessary. As attested by the size of our DQ5 database, the assessment process works and needs no major changes at this time.

In this research study, we improve upon the original *Changing Roles* research. This study includes two major improvements. First, the expanded interview process includes senior executives and line managers outside of the financial organization. Second, the individual case studies are written from a management perspective, not a financial perspective. Our goal is to describe and explain how the financial organization's practices fit into a firm's overall management operating philosophy.

In Chapter 1, we begin the process by describing the conceptual framework used to conduct the management interviews and write each firm's case study.

Endnotes

1. *Changing Roles of Financial Management,* Financial Executives Research Foundation, 1990.

2. The six firms included in the original study were AT&T, Boeing, Citicorp, Ford, Merck, and 3M.

3. *Business Advocate or Corporate Policeman?: Assessing Your Role as a Financial Executive,* Financial Executives Research Foundation, 1993. The original diagnostic questionnaire (DQ) was administered to 805 managers (297 financial managers and 508 nonfinancial managers).

4. This discussion is based on the responses of the original 805 managers as well as the 2,400 responses to the current version of the questionnaire (831 financial managers and 1,569 nonfinancial managers).

5. The initial distribution of scores was based on the orientation receiving the highest number of responses falling under the competitive-team, command-and-control, and conformance orientations. The command-and-control responses were identified with the Business Advocate and Corporate Policeman models based on the orientation receiving the second-highest score.

6. The comparison is based on the responses of over 1,500 nonfinancial managers who have completed the current version of our diagnostic questionnaire.

1

The Evolution of Financial Management: Strategy, Control, Accountability, and Culture

The current research study has been designed to go beyond the findings summarized in the Introduction. In particular, we wanted to minimize the effects of a possible "rhetoric/reality" gap between the perceptions that financial managers have of themselves and the perceptions that nonfinancial managers have of financial managers. The only way we could see to do this was to include nonfinancial managers in this research project.

The findings reported in this study are based on the following interview protocol, which was followed at each of the case-study firms. Interviews were conducted with

1. The CEO and other members of the senior management team, to get their views on how financial people are contributing to the overall success of the firm;

2. Operating managers in the business units involved with key management initiatives, to spell out, in some detail, how financial people are contributing to the success of these business operations; and

3. The CFO and key members of his or her management team, along with financial managers working within the business units or on key business initiatives.

Consistent with the research methodology we employed in the original *Changing Roles* research, all the findings reported in this study have been reviewed and approved by each firm.

The five firms that agreed to participate in this study are Applied Materials, Inc., BellSouth Corporation, The Boeing Company, Caterpillar Inc., and Nucor Corp. In the spirit of full disclosure, each firm that was invited to participate in this study had the opportunity to review

1. Our past research findings, as presented in the Introduction (as well as the original research monographs),

2. A copy of the interview protocol that we would be using in the management interviews,[1] and

3. The conceptual framework that we would be using to tell each firm's story and summarize what we found in the interviews across all five firms.

In the remainder of this chapter, we will use selected findings from the research interviews at all five firms to illustrate the conceptual framework. This framework will then serve as the common touchstone for each of the case studies.

The Conceptual Framework

Our work in executive management programs has shown us that managers have a very healthy appetite for financial information. They want to satisfy their hunger in order to become better managers, but most nonfinancial managers do not want to overeat. At some point in their careers, they decided that they did not want to pursue a career in finance.

Whether these managers come from Business Advocate or Corporate Policeman environments, they know that their business unit's performance and the performance of the entire firm is measured in financial terms. They realize that they need to know more about how they can have a positive impact on the financial performance of their firm. They just want to acquire that knowledge without having to become accountants. To their minds, the whole purpose of forming business teams is to be able to draw on another team member's expertise (e.g., marketing, finance, production, management information systems (MIS), human resources (HR), procurement) without having to become experts in that field themselves.

To help managers develop a better understanding of their business through financial information, we begin by talking about a business strategy, management control, and corporate accountability loop. At every level within the organization, managers are charged with implementing some aspect of the firm's overall business strategy. And to be effective, that strategy must consider the needs of all the firm's stakeholders (including customers, suppliers, employees, lenders, and shareholders).

The effects of trying to implement that business strategy, along with the effects of other economic events over which management has no control, are then captured in the firm's management control system—in particular, the firm's accounting system. Formal accountability for the financial performance of the business units and the entire firm is then communicated to internal and external stakeholders through annual, quarterly, and monthly financial statements.

Formal accountability through financial statements provides a common denominator for all firms. In a very real sense, all firms whose stock is publicly traded must conform to generally accepted accounting principles (GAAP) when preparing financial statements for external parties. Business Advocates have to conform to the same GAAP as do Corporate Policemen.

What distinguishes Business Advocates from Corporate Policemen is the emphasis on *substantive* accountability. In a Business Advocate environment, the financial organization and financial people exist to help managers and employees make their firm more successful. They play an active role in helping the business units achieve their strategic objectives, in helping their firms create shareholder value, and in business strategy, management control, and corporate accountability.

Given this more active involvement in the business, two questions need to be answered:

1. What responsibilities do financial people in Business Advocate environments take on when they become more involved in the business?

2. Do financial people in Business Advocate environments take on the same responsibilities in different firms, or do their responsibilities differ across firms?

In the course of our visits to the case-study firms, it became evident that financial people in Business Advocate environments take on more management responsibilities, but these responsibilities vary across firms. The interaction among strategy, control, and accountability plays out in different ways in different firm cultures. Without some understanding of a firm's culture, it would be almost impossible to understand how financial people make a substantive contribution to the firm's success. To a certain extent, culture was the missing link in the original *Changing Roles* research.

Figure 1.1 presents the conceptual framework that resulted from adding culture to the strategy, control, and accountability loop. Even though entire treatises have been written about each of the elements in the conceptual framework, we believe that all of the elements have to be studied as a single system. As we shall see, the cultures at Applied Materials, BellSouth, Boeing, Caterpillar, and Nucor have a significant impact on the CFO's role and the roles of all the financial people in the firm.

In the remainder of this chapter, we will flesh out the conceptual framework by referring to the individual case studies. However, before we proceed, we think it is important to highlight one of the threads that was woven across all five firms.

FIGURE 1.1   The Business Advocate Perspective:
Strategy, Control, Accountability, and Culture

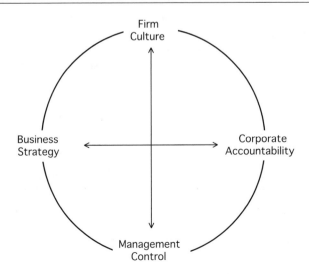

In each of the case-study firms, we found that executives and managers with financial backgrounds were being asked to step into broader management roles. Financial people with interests that go beyond straight accounting and finance were being asked to assume broader management responsibilities. Terms like "business-unit CFO," "vice president for business resources," or "division business manager" were used to describe these expanded roles. The names varied from firm to firm, but the job descriptions were similar.

Financial people who preferred to remain wedded to their functional or technical expertise were not considered for key management positions. The people who were advancing within their organizations had to demonstrate strong interpersonal and communication skills to become business managers.

Corporate Themes

The value of a conceptual framework lies in its ability to help identify common themes that exist across firms yet allow for unique differences to surface for individual firms. We expected to hear different stories across firms owing to industry differences (semiconductor fabrication equipment, telecommunications, aerospace, heavy equipment, and steel). It was only through the interview process that we could identify a set of common themes that would enable us to tie all five firms together.

Figure 1.2 divides the conceptual framework into four quadrants with a single theme identified with each quadrant.

When managers talk about their firm's culture, they are talking about the human side of the enterprise—about people, about the stakeholders in the firm. The internal stakeholders are the employees and managers. We use the theme "workforce" to refer to issues affecting employees and managers. The primary external stakeholders in the firm are suppliers, customers, shareholders, regulators, and financial analysts. We use the theme "market" to refer to issues affecting these external stakeholders.

When executives talk about changing their firm's culture, they mean changing the ways internal and external stakeholders will behave in the future. As we shall see in each of the case studies, talking about changing the firm's culture is one thing. Actually changing the culture is quite another. Cultures cannot be changed overnight.

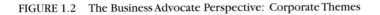

FIGURE 1.2   The Business Advocate Perspective: Corporate Themes

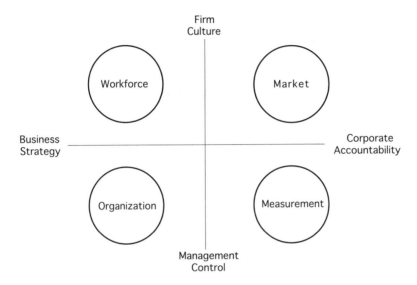

When managers talk about management control, they talk about those business practices that keep the firm from "flying apart." The two management controls that managers consider most important are the firm's organizational structure and its measurement system.

We use the theme "organization" to refer to issues affecting how the firm is structured to achieve its business objectives. We use the theme "measurement" to refer to issues affecting the collection and reporting of information for management control.

As we can see from Figure 1.2, issues involving business strategy and management control are related to how the firm is organized to achieve its business objectives. Issues involving management control and corporate accountability are related to the firm's measurement practices. Issues involving corporate accountability and firm culture are related to the market. And issues involving firm culture and business strategy are related to the workforce.

We will illustrate the issues that surfaced around each of the corporate themes during management interviews by reference to the findings reported in the individual case studies.

Business Strategy and Management Control

At each of the firms, the common theme that links business strategy to management control is *organization.*

Nucor

Of all the firms participating in this study, Nucor has maintained the most stable organizational structure. Nucor is organized into autonomous divisions with only four management levels in its entire management hierarchy. That particular organizational structure has been in place since the late 1960s, when Nucor was born out of the ashes of the old Nuclear Corporation of America. In the Nucor system, controllers function as business unit CFOs to vice presidents and general managers of their divisions.

Because the division controllers are so integrated into the business operations at Nucor, we found it hard to talk about a separate financial "organization." As we shall see, Nucor practices "lean administration." The costs associated with maintaining a separate financial organization would only get in the way of Nucor's objective of being the least cost producer of high-quality steel.

Caterpillar

During the early 1990s, Caterpillar went through a major reorganization. Until that time, Caterpillar was a functionally oriented, bureaucratic organization with all decision making centralized in the executive offices. Caterpillar is now organized into 17 product divisions and 5 support service divisions. As one of the five support service divisions, the financial organization has to recover its costs through billings to the profit center divisions. As customers, the profit center divisions do not have to purchase the services they need from the financial organization. As we shall see in the Caterpillar story, the size, status, and rewards accruing to the support service divisions are directly related to their ability to provide high-quality services to their internal (and external) customers.

Applied Materials

Since Jim Morgan arrived 20 years ago, emphasis has been placed on the need for a very strong, independent financial organization. The CFO has been charged with making sure that there were no financial "surprises" as the company grew at a compound growth rate of 31 percent a year over the past 20 years. With some product groups having annual revenues of more than $1.0 billion (approximating the total revenues for the entire company in fiscal year 1993), senior management is faced with the challenge of developing a "partnership" between the financial organization and the business units.

BellSouth

When the holding company for BellSouth Enterprises (BSE) was combined with the holding company for the BellSouth Corporation, financial people experienced with the unregulated side of the business assumed the majority of the corporate positions. Under the direction of the corporate CFO, BellSouth is infusing the financial discipline used to run the unregulated side of the business (BSE) into BellSouth Telecommunications (BST), the regulated side of the business. Much of the BellSouth story revolves around defining the role of the business-unit CFOs on the regulated side of the business and going outside BellSouth to hire people who can fill those positions.

Boeing

Boeing wants to be known as a world-class, efficient manufacturing company rather than an engineering and technology company, at least on the commercial side of the business. Efficiency implies responsibility for keeping costs under control. The position of vice president of business resources has been created for both the commercial and defense and space sides of Boeing. The finance directors who previously reported to the presidents of the businesses now report to the vice presidents of business resources.

Management Control and Corporate Accountability

The common theme that links a firm's management control system to corporate accountability is *measurement.*

Caterpillar

The primary measure of financial success at Caterpillar is return on assets (ROA). Don Fites, Caterpillar's CEO (and architect of the corporate reorganization in 1990), credits the ROA-based financial measurement system designed by the corporate accounting group with helping make Caterpillar's reorganization a success. The division and corporate ROA measures are all integrated into Caterpillar's incentive compensation programs.

Nucor

At the production group level, the chief measure of success is prime (quality) tons of steel produced. At the division level, ROA is a primary measure of financial success. At the senior officer level, the primary measure of success is return on equity (ROE). All the measures of success are tied directly to one of the company's four incentive compensation programs.

Senior executives at both Caterpillar and Nucor believe that the best way to keep people focused on the business is to use simple, straightforward measures of success and reward people for accomplishing their production, ROA, and ROE goals.

As managers at both firms reiterated time and again, with ROA as your primary measure of success (or one of the primary measures), you can only do two things to increase your ROA: increase earnings, reduce assets, or do a little of both.

As we shall see in the context of their individual case studies, their management control systems have been designed to give all employees timely feedback on how well they are doing in meeting their ROA objectives.

Applied Materials

Return on operating assets is an important performance measure at Applied Materials, although margin management (market share, sales, expense control, and profit margins) is currently given higher priority than asset management (inventory, receivables, and facilities). As Applied Materials attempts to combine its emphasis on technological innovation with a focus on operational excellence, asset management is receiving more attention from senior management.

Boeing

The primary financial measure at Boeing is shareholder value (as measured by dividends plus stock price appreciation). Internally, shareholder value translates into discounted cash flows. Boeing found that discounted cash flow was more closely tied to shareholder value than to ROE, the primary measure of financial performance until 1996.

BellSouth

The primary financial measures at BellSouth are earnings and cash flow. ROA and ROE are currently being deemphasized because of how these measures were used to run the business in a regulated world. Earnings and cash flow measures are believed to be more consistent with competitive, market-based planning.

Corporate Accountability and Firm Culture

The common theme that links corporate accountability to the firm culture is the *market.* When firms talk about the market, they either talk about "customer" markets or "capital" markets—typically one or the other, but not both.

Applied Materials

It is important to increase market share by being first to market with the right technology at Applied Materials. Sales may be growing faster or slower than originally forecast, but managers know they had better be trying to increase their position relative to the competition, irrespective of changes in the overall economy. Managers can "get called out on the carpet" for product portfolio or market share issues.

Nucor

At Nucor, the name of the game is to grow the business by taking market share away from the competition. In a relatively stable U.S. market for steel (110 million tons per year), you take market share away from the competition through lower prices. You can lower prices and still be profitable at the bottom of the business cycle if you are the low-cost producer.

Caterpillar

Many of the changes that have occurred at Caterpillar since the early 1980s can be traced back to its Japanese competition. A benchmarking study performed by the corporate accounting group helped Caterpillar realize that it had a "30 percent cost problem" relative to its Japanese competition. To a certain extent, everything Caterpillar has accomplished over the past 17 years has been part of the solution to this competitive cost problem.

Executives and managers at Applied Materials, Nucor, and Caterpillar believe that shareholders will receive their just rewards in the capital marketplace if managers do their job in satisfying their customers.

BellSouth

After being divested from AT&T, BellSouth began to develop a sense of how to compete in the marketplace through BellSouth Enterprises, the unregulated side of the business. The corporate financial organization is currently employing the expertise it developed through its merger and acquisition activities to translate "shareholder expectations" (for dividends and stock price appreciation) to help managers on the regulated side of the business develop a market orientation.

Boeing

The management interviews at Boeing focused more on capital markets than on customer markets. The corporate financial group was particularly interested in how financial analysts and investors looked at their firm. They talked in terms of "shareholder expectations" for dividends and stock price appreciation. They also stressed how the market discounts expected future cash flows in arriving at a price for Boeing common stock. In both firms, the corporate financial people used "market expectations" to set earnings and cash flow targets for the business units.

Firm Culture and Business Strategy

The common theme that links the firm's culture to business strategy is the *workforce.*

Nucor

In Nucor, employee relations are based on four clear-cut principles:

1. Management is obligated to manage Nucor in such a way that employees will have the opportunity to earn according to their productivity.

2. Employees should feel confident that if they do their jobs properly, they will have a job tomorrow.

3. Employees have the right to be treated fairly and must believe that they will be.

4. Employees must have an avenue of appeal when they believe they are being treated unfairly.[2]

From a financial perspective, these four principles translate into a culture of open communications. Of all the firms included in this study, Nucor shared the most financial information with all employees.

Caterpillar

Caterpillar is committed to improving the business competency of all employees (managers, salaried workers, and hourly employees). The corporate accounting group has developed a set of five business games that it uses to teach the financial concepts that senior management uses to run the business: the accounting game, the accountability game, the cash flow game, the cost connection game, and the foreign currency game.

Boeing

Boeing is just starting to create instructional materials similar to the business games developed at Caterpillar. The responsibility for developing business competency within the workforce has been assigned to the Boeing Center for Leadership and Learning (BCLL). Since BCLL is recognized worldwide for its customer pilot and maintenance crew training programs, Phil Condit, Boeing's CEO, tapped the head of BCLL to spearhead the development of business competence within Boeing's workforce.

As Caterpillar already knows, and as Boeing is finding out, the explicit commitment to improve the business competence of all employees puts pressure on the financial organization to share more information. Efforts to improve business competence without information sharing and open communications are a waste of money. From our research perspective, Boeing is starting to move closer to Caterpillar, and Caterpillar is moving closer to Nucor in terms of employee relations.

BellSouth

At BellSouth, the workforce issues are at a more basic economic level. Over the past several years, management has been involved in downsizing the organization and identifying the new skill sets managers need to operate in a competitive environment instead of a regulatory environment. As discussed more fully within the context of the BellSouth story, financial skills steeped in a regulatory accounting tradition are ill-suited for working in a competitive environment.

Applied Materials

If BellSouth is downsizing, Applied Materials is upsizing. Because of the financial organization's reputation for hiring highly qualified people, the product groups are "raiding" the financial organization to meet their needs for qualified managers. At $4.1 billion plus in 1996 revenues and with significant growth opportunities over the next several years, Applied Materials is devoting more resources to developing the human resources side of the business at both the corporate and product division levels.

As mentioned previously, our objectives in this study are twofold: to go beyond the findings reported in the original *Changing Roles* research, and to tell each firm's story from a management perspective. By using the corporate themes to tell a story about each firm, we were able to take a first step toward achieving our objectives. However, we needed to take one additional step to pull together, or integrate, the issues surrounding the corporate themes at each firm.

Integrating Mechanisms

In the process of describing the major themes that link strategy to control to accountability and to culture, we discovered another set of linkages or integrating mechanisms that exist at some or all of the case-study firms.

Figure 1.3 presents the four integrating mechanisms we use to link the corporate themes to tell a unified story about each firm.

The organization exists in isolation from the measurement system. Firms are, or should be, organized to achieve an optimal level of performance. The purpose of a firm's measurement system is to measure that performance. Measurement systems, or scorekeeping systems, are designed to provide managers, employees, and external parties with feedback about the firm's performance. Performance is therefore the mechanism that integrates the organization with the measurement system.

The organization exists in isolation from the workforce. Without a skilled and dedicated workforce, the best organizational structure that consultants can design is unlikely to produce the financial results that senior executives expect. Compensation is the mechanism that integrates the workforce with the organization.

Without financial information about the firm's performance, mangers, employees, shareholders, financial analysts, and other stakeholders have no way of knowing how well the firm is doing. Are managers growing their business in terms of increasing sales? Are they growing earnings even though they are not increasing sales? Is management growing earnings per share? Are managers increasing their market share?

FIGURE 1.3 The Business Advocate Perspective:
Corporate Themes and Integrating Mechanisms

Without some form of growth, the market value of a firm's common stock is not likely to increase. Growth is therefore the mechanism that integrates the measurement system with the market.

Finally, the workforce exists in isolation from the market. Virtually every proxy statement of publicly held firms includes a section about the firm's executive compensation program. In order to align the interests of senior executives with the interests of shareholders, these executives receive stock options and restricted stock awards based on the firm's financial performance. Some plans also include a requirement that managers own a prescribed number of shares of common stock in the firm based on their annual compensation. Other firms have extended the opportunity to become shareholders to all employees. Ownership is therefore the mechanism that integrates the workforce with the market.

These integrating mechanisms represent the glue that holds the framework together. This glue makes the whole greater than the sum of its parts.

Performance

Performance integrates the organization with the measurement system. In each of the case-study firms, a few basic performance measures provide the mechanism for integrating the organization with the measurement system.

At Nucor, Applied Materials, and Caterpillar, performance provides a strong link between the organization and the measurement system.

Nucor

At Nucor, performance is defined in terms of tons of prime (high-quality) steel produced by each division. Part of Nucor's overall business strategy is to be the least cost steel producer in America. To increase market share even in a down market, management wants to be able to make a profit at the bottom of the business cycle. The way to do that is to be the least cost producer. In that way, Nucor can cut price, keep employees working, and still make money for its shareholders. The ROA and ROE measurement systems are based on the primary performance measure, prime tons of steel produced.

Applied Materials

At Applied Materials, performance in the business units is defined in terms of market share, revenues, expenses, and profits. The company is in the process of transferring a more complete ownership of the asset side of the balance sheet to the business units and increasing the emphasis of asset management in the definition of business-unit performance.

Caterpillar

At Caterpillar, the fundamental performance measures are "accountable profit" and "accountable assets." Each division manager and the product managers within each division are held accountable for their own bottom line and ROA. Through a system of market-based transfer pricing, every manager is held accountable for his or her revenues, expenses, and assets employed in the business. No corporate costs are allocated to the business units, and all service centers have to recover their costs by selling their services to the business units. The ROA-based measurement system supports the performance concepts of accountable profit and accountable assets.

Boeing

As Boeing, performance is defined internally in terms of operating earnings and discounted cash flow. Efforts are under way to reconcile the differences between how performance is defined for internal and external reporting purposes.

BellSouth

BellSouth defines financial performance in terms of earnings and cash flow. A "gap" exists currently between the performance measures BellSouth has been using in the past and the performance measures it wants to use in the future. The company is broadening its use of profit centers.

Compensation

Compensation integrates the organization with the workforce. There is no question that compensation is the glue that binds people to the organization. Unless employees are paid adequately, such issues as job security, loyalty, mutual respect, and trust have little meaning.

Nucor and Caterpillar

At Nucor, every employee is on some sort of incentive compensation plan. Production employees receive a bonus based on the amount of prime tons produced. Their bonuses are paid weekly. Plant managers and staff personnel receive an annual bonus based on the division's ROA. The incentive compensation of senior executives (17 in all) is based on ROE after a minimum earnings target has been exceeded. Nucor's program is based on the principle of "share the pain, share the gain."

At Caterpillar, managers, salaried employees, and some hourly employees have some portion of their pay at risk. As at Nucor, incentive compensation is linked to performance and monitored through the measurement system. As we shall see in the Caterpillar story, incentive compensation is not the same as profit sharing.

Tying incentive pay to performance through the way the company is organized represents an important part of both the Nucor and Caterpillar stories.

BellSouth, Boeing, and Applied Materials

At BellSouth, Boeing, and Applied Materials, incentive compensation typically is limited to the managers in the executive compensation groups.

Incentive compensation was not a major topic of discussion in the management interviews.

Growth

Growth integrates the measurement system with the market. In the interviews with senior executives, growing the business by selling more products, acquiring other companies, or going into joint ventures were all topics of immediate concern. Every senior executive we interviewed was concerned with growing the business and creating shareholder value. The real question was how each firm was going about growing its business without diluting the return on the shareholders' investment.

Applied Materials

As mentioned previously, Applied Materials has grown at a 31 percent compound growth rate for the past 20 years. As the company attempts to balance growth execution, managers are placing more emphasis on cost control and increased asset utilization.

Nucor

At Nucor, management keeps its growth policy simple. Existing divisions are expected to grow sales and increase earnings by increasing productivity. Capital expenditures equal to the annual depreciation charges are used to upgrade facilities and fund productivity improvements. New facilities are built out of earnings and new borrowings. Nucor's policy is to stay at or below a 30 percent debt-to-equity ratio in growing the business.

Caterpillar

Since the company reorganized in 1990, growth at Caterpillar has meant "earnings growth." Caterpillar's goal until about a year ago was to increase earnings by reducing costs while not increasing the asset base. With that goal pretty much accomplished, Caterpillar is looking for new growth opportunities that will allow the company to grow the total return to shareholders faster than the growth of the S&P 500 Index.

Boeing

Anyone who has even glanced at a business periodical within the past year knows that Boeing has more than doubled the size of its business through the acquisition of Rockwell International's defense and space business and the acquisition of McDonnell Douglas. As these new acquisitions are being integrated into Boeing, management is trying to grow earnings and cash flows in existing businesses through cost control.

BellSouth

Ever since BellSouth was created in the split-up of AT&T, BellSouth Enterprises has been the company's "growth engine." BellSouth has grown its cellular business and its international operations primarily through acquisitions. In its core telecommunications business it has concentrated on "growing earnings" through marketing new and existing services, downsizing, and cost control. With most of the downsizing completed, BellSouth is looking for growth opportunities in the long-distance business and its core local service businesses.

Ownership

Ownership links the workforce to the market. It is one thing to talk about "thinking like owners" or instilling "a sense of ownership" among employees. It is quite another to actually be an owner of stock in the corporation. Talk is cheap. Actions are what count.

In all five firms, senior managers participate in some form of incentive plan involving stock options or restricted stock awards. In Caterpillar's case, senior managers are also required to own shares of stock equal to one-third, or 33 percent, of the stock options granted within the past three years. As in other major U.S. corporations, the interests of senior managers have been aligned with the interests of the shareholders through stock ownership.

All five firms had some form of profit-sharing and stock-ownership programs for employees other than executives. However, except for Boeing, these programs were more or less incidental to the firm's overall business strategy.

Boeing

Probably the most innovative program for linking employees to the capital market was implemented by Boeing during the summer of 1996. Boeing established a $1 billion trust fund for its employees. Called the ShareValue program, it covers all employees not covered in the executive compensation program. At the program's inception, Boeing invested $1 billion in Boeing common stock. Every two years, employees will receive a payout in stock or cash based on the total return (dividends plus stock price appreciation) on the $1 billion investment. Because the incentive compensation of senior managers is also based on the total return to shareholders, Boeing has aligned the interests of shareholders with those of senior management and has aligned the interests of its employees with those of senior management and the shareholders.

The Role of the Financial Organization

In using the conceptual framework as a touchstone for telling a story about each firm, we will see that the contribution of financial organization and financial people must be described within the context of their firm's culture. We have chosen to expand the business strategy, management control, and corporate accountability loop to include the firm's culture. As we shall see, the Business Advocate model of financial management plays out somewhat differently in each culture.

Financial people are most integrated into the business at Caterpillar and Nucor. The Caterpillar and Nucor stories focus on how the financial organization and financial people have already contributed to the success of both firms. Nucor's culture has remained virtually the same since Ken Iverson and Sam Siegel took control of the company in the mid-1960s. Caterpillar's culture has remained virtually the same since Don Fites became CEO and reorganized the company in the early 1990s. The culture at Applied Materials has remained virtually the same ever since Jim Morgan became CEO in the late 1970s, although that culture is beginning to change as the company grows.

The cultures at both BellSouth and Boeing are in transition. At BellSouth, the executive vice president and CFO is in the process of changing the culture on the regulated side of the business to be more like the culture on the unregulated side. At Boeing, the CEO is doing double duty. On the one hand, he is trying to change the company from a technology-driven company to a manufacturing company. On the other hand, he must integrate the Boeing and McDonnell Douglas cultures into a single culture.

The next five chapters contain the individual case studies, presented in the following order: Caterpillar, Nucor, BellSouth, Boeing, and Applied Materials. The Caterpillar and Nucor stories exemplify the Business Advocate model of financial management in actual practice. The BellSouth, Boeing, and Applied Materials stories exemplify firms moving toward the Business Advocate model. BellSouth is trying to make the transition to the Business Advocate model in anticipation of the type of financial skills the company will need in competitive (as opposed to regulated) markets. Boeing is making the move to the Business Advocate model to align the commitment to increasing shareholder value with a new internal performance measurement system that emphasizes operating earnings and cash flow measures. Applied Materials is making the move to the Business Advocate model in an effort to "strategically align" the financial organization with the needs of its internal customers, the business units.

In the final chapter, we attempt to draw some overall conclusions about how the five case-study firms have moved from a commitment to the Business Advocate model of financial management to developing the capabilities to make the model a reality.

The BellSouth story is one-half accomplishment (on the unregulated side of the business) and one-half work in progress (on the regulated side of the business). The Boeing and Applied Materials stories are mostly works in progress. At these firms, most of the management interviews focused on how senior management wanted the financial organization to evolve.

Endnotes

1. A copy of the interview protocol is presented in the appendix.

2. *The Nucor Story,* p. 6.

2
Caterpillar Inc.

In a very real sense, the changes that Caterpillar has undergone since the early 1980s reflect the broader transformation of American industry. The combination of the threat posed by Japanese competition and the $953 million in losses incurred from 1982 through 1984 made it very clear that the company could not continue to do business in the future as it had in the past.

Even though Caterpillar was the global leader in its industry, the company was not making money. An analysis of its main Japanese competitor, Komatsu, showed Caterpillar that it had a 30 percent "cost problem." It was one thing to be able to charge a price premium for superior service and support. It was quite another to charge a premium that would also cover the 30 percent cost problem.

As in the Ford story we told back in 1990,[1] many of the management changes that have occurred at Caterpillar can be traced back to the competition from Japan and the 30 percent cost problem.[2] From that starting point, the Caterpillar story can be told in terms of a series of milestones that capture the most dramatic events affecting the company. As we shall see, the financial organization, and the Corporate Accounting group in particular, has played an integral role in Caterpillar's transformation.

In one of our initial interviews at Caterpillar, Lou Jones, Cost Management and Business Services Manager (with 44 years of experience), gave us the following brief history of the company before we started the management interviews. Several of the major milestones proved invaluable in developing the Caterpillar story.

1. In 1985/86, we introduced the Plant with a Future (PWAF) program to help solve our cost problem. We spent about $1.8 billion in capital and $1 billion on start-up costs to modernize our plants. The PWAF program was completed in the early 1990s.

2. In 1990, we reorganized the company. We went from being a highly centralized, functional organization to a decentralized, customer-focused organization. The company was initially reorganized into 14 profit center divisions and 4 service center divisions.

3. Within six months of reorganizing the company, we introduced a new measurement system tied directly to the new organizational structure. We called the measurement system the "accountable profit" system. In the new organization, managers were going to be held accountable for the profit they generated and the capital they employed to generate that profit. ROA was chosen as the financial performance metric to link the measurement system to the new organizational structure.

4. In 1991, we introduced the incentive compensation system for the managers and salaried workers in the profit centers. At that time, a percentage of every manager's and salaried worker's salary became "at risk." The pay at risk was tied primarily to the financial performance of the particular profit center and the overall corporate ROA.

5. In 1993, we introduced incentive compensation to the managers and salaried workers in the service divisions.

6. With accountabilities established and performance measurements and the incentive compensation system in place, the business units developed business strategies. These strategies included a vision, mission, critical issues, and critical success factors. Many business units also developed a set of common values to form the framework for managing the business and building relationships.[3]

To a certain extent, this brief history tells all there is to tell about Caterpillar. For managers who have worked at Caterpillar for most of their professional lives, like Lou Jones, each milestone conjures up a host of memories and experiences. For researchers like ourselves, this brief history provided the context for making sense of what we heard in management interviews.

If we cast these same events within the context of the conceptual model introduced in Chapter 1, the Caterpillar story may be visualized as shown in Figure 2.1.

FIGURE 2.1   Caterpillar: The Business Advocate Perspective—
Corporate Themes and Integrating Mechanisms

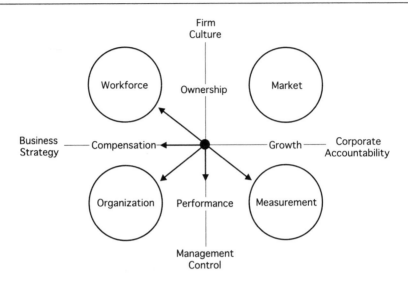

Simply stated, Caterpillar has developed a management operating philosophy that focuses on performance and compensation. Managers are held accountable for their performance, and performance is measured in terms of ROA. ROA is also a key component of Caterpillar's incentive compensation system. Some portion of every manager's annual incentive compensation (and employees' incentive compensation where implemented) is based on meeting division and corporate ROA targets. At Caterpillar, if you have the right organization, the right measurement system, and the right reward system for the workforce, the company will be doing the right thing for its customers and shareholders.

Let the Story Begin

Over the past decade, Caterpillar has created a decentralized, market-focused organization built around profit center divisions and service center divisions.[4] To make this new organization work as designed, Caterpillar developed a measurement system based on the concepts of accountable profit and accountable assets. ROA was chosen, and continues to be the key performance indicator that links the organization to the measurement system.

With the new organization and measurement system in place, Caterpillar concentrated on changing its compensation system to link pay more closely to performance. Under the new incentive compensation system, all managers and salaried employees have some amount of their pay at risk. All employees included in the incentive compensation system have part of their pay at risk based on achieving (1) the business unit's ROA target, (2) the corporate ROA target, and (3) individual and business-unit initiatives.

If the financial people at Caterpillar, specifically the accounting people, were typical "bean counters," we might expect them to play some role in helping to develop the new measurement system, and we would be right. However, as we shall see, the accounting group has played a major part in all aspects of Caterpillar's transformation. In fact, the role of accounting within Caterpillar has increased in prominence. At Caterpillar, accounting people enjoy their role as business partners.

In telling the Caterpillar story, we will go back to several years before the reorganization to understand why the reorganization was deemed necessary. Although the initial changes in response to the Japanese competition and the 30 percent cost problem had a number of positive effects, these changes still needed to be incorporated into a new decentralized business organization.

We begin the Caterpillar story with the PWAF program.

Plant With a Future

In 1983, Caterpillar's first response to meeting the Japanese competition was to reorganize the marketing organization to increase customer focus. The "customers" in this case were the 200 dealers who sold Caterpillar products to end users. These 200 dealers were the ones who had to compete head to head with the Japanese.

From the dealers' perspective, Caterpillar had two major problems: The product development cycle was too long, and costs were too high. Even though Caterpillar could charge a premium based on product support, product quality, and residual value of the equipment, the premium had to be in line with the prices charged by the Japanese. The PWAF program was designed to help solve the cost problem.

PWAF provided a process and technological solution to the cost problem, but it did not address the organizational problems associated with a highly centralized, functional organization. As Lou Jones explains,

> PWAF was designed to give us an absolutely streamlined, synchronous flow-type manufacturing process without the waste and inefficiencies that go with storing inventory and moving materials to locations all over the factory floor. We improved throughput through the factory. We improved asset management by purchasing machines that were very flexible and reducing set-up times for all equipment. It is now two or three hours of set-up or no set-up time at all. We now run daily batch sizes. We run to meet the assembly line for the next day.

Within each plant, PWAF helped reduce costs and improve asset management. However, the cost problems associated with transfers between plants often fell through the cracks, as illustrated by the story of the "traveling gear" as told by Mark Thompson, Business Analysis Manager:

> There was a gear that came into our [Aurora, Illinois] factory to be machined. After machining, it was put back in inventory before being shipped to Joliet [Illinois] for heat treatment. It was then sent back to the original supplier for some finishing work and then sent to Decatur [Illinois]. This gear traveled 300 miles, and it took six to eight weeks to get into the final product.
>
> We don't do that anymore. We have really streamlined the manufacturing process to reduce unnecessary steps and reduce our investment in inventory. We have increased inventory turns and eliminated our non-value-added work that goes along with our old ways of doing business.
>
> Under our old organization, the corporate group owned the inventory. We would transfer the finished product to corporate, and it would not even be on our general ledger. We were a cost center, pure and simple.

We have found that sharing the traveling gear story with managers in executive education programs creates an immediate bond within the group. It is sort of like sharing a wilderness adventure to develop a sense of camaraderie without having to go outside. Virtually everyone in these executive programs has a version of the traveling gear story. Within any company, technical solutions to problems can only go so far. At some point, management must address the organizational issues that affect performance. In Caterpillar's case, senior management made the decision to reorganize the company around customers and product groups. The highly centralized functional organization had to be replaced by a decentralized customer-focused organization that was responsive, flexible, and versatile.

The Functional Organization

When managers at Caterpillar talked about the previous functional organization, they spoke from experience. Since most of the senior managers we interviewed had more than 25 years with the company, they all had worked within that functional organization. And the best way to describe that experience is through their own words. Ron Bonati, Vice President, explains,

> We had a "severally responsible" organization. Everybody was responsible, but nobody was responsible. We had functionalism in its most elaborate form. We had an engineering chimney, a manufacturing chimney, a marketing chimney, an accounting chimney, and a finance chimney. Movement across chimneys rarely, if ever, happened. Each group was looking at the business through a very functional set of eyeballs, and I think it became abundantly clear to a lot of people around here that this was not going to work in the future. We needed to take a broader view of the business, and in order to do that, we had to mix and match people, and that's happened big time.

Jim Baldwin, Vice President, adds,

> Under the old functional organization, I was an inventory control manager where service was the only thing people talked about. Inventory levels, the dollars tied up in inventory, were only things financial people talked about. Pricing was in the financial organization. Until 1990, both machine and parts pricing were controlled at the corporate level. Now the pricing is part of the profit center manager's responsibility.

> In the old days, if it wasn't your responsibility, you just focused on service. Service was everything. Service is still everything, but you have to continue to balance it with your assets. Assets were free. Now we get charged a cost of capital on our inventory investment.

Gary Stroup, Vice President, continues,

> Prior to the reorganization, we were cost centers. I was judged against a departmental expense statement. I was a cost center. I was a cost manager. We would put together a departmental expense budget and get it approved. We were experts at convincing management that it was a perfect budget, and it had a lot of stretch in it. Once it was approved, my whole line-of-sight management, my whole concern, my whole system of measurements,

was staying within that budget. I was going to be judged on whether I hit that departmental expense target or I didn't.

Gary Stroup uses the term "line-of-sight management" to describe how he viewed the world under the old functional organization. As it turns out, the use of this term is pervasive throughout Caterpillar. You focus your line of sight on what you are responsible for and what you will be held accountable for. In order to do their own jobs, middle managers had to assume that senior managers knew what they were doing, even though this approach to management might not make a lot of sense to them. As Stroup explains,

> If the company was going into the tank, I could put blinders on and say, "Hey, that's somebody else's problem. That's the executive office's problem." My problem is to stay within my budget, and by gosh, come the end of the year, I am like the military, I am going to do whatever I have to to hit that budget. If I have to spend a little money, I will because I will lose that money next year. And if I hit that budget, my plant manager could be over there wringing his hands about how we were going to make money with that, but he would come back and rate me outstanding because I hit my budget, and I felt good. I'd read the paper and see that Caterpillar was in trouble, but I'd feel good because I did my job.

Bonati adds,

> Back in the old days when I was growing up in the marketing division, I didn't care about the financing thing. Nobody ever tried to explain it to me. I didn't know what our margins were; in fact, it was almost a secret. So if you aren't going to tell me about it, I don't care. If you're not going to share the margin information with me, fine with me. I don't worry about it then. I will sell as many products at a discount as I can in order to make my market-share objectives.

> We all know that you would not run your own business that way. That isn't the way you'd run any business. You would want to sell as many as you can, but you sure are going to make some money from it. And to know that, you better know how much you are making on each one. But we didn't used to share that information. It really was secret.

In telling the Caterpillar story, the intensity of the frustration with the old functional organization cannot be ignored. And what is really interesting is that the people running Caterpillar today are the same ones who lived through the previous functional organization. They are the ones who knew that there must be a better way of running the business.

The Product Control Group

In a highly centralized organization, the only place all of the functions come together is at the top. In Caterpillar's case, the product control group was charged with the responsibility of bringing all of the functions together. Dan Murphy, Vice President, says,

> I worked in Decatur for seven years and then moved to the product control group in Peoria. That group was responsible for bringing manufacturing, engineering, marketing, and finance together to create a business plan. In that group, you were a referee and you wore a striped shirt and a whistle.
>
> It was an exercise in spear catching. We were the peacekeepers between the functions. We were the ones who uploaded the proposals to the executive office.

Glen Barton, Group President, adds,

> I moved on to the product control group, where we tried to get the functions to talk to each other in the product development process, particularly when the projects required capital expenditures. The product control group was multidisciplinary even though it was always headed by a marketing guy. It was a good assignment for tracking good people. You developed a good understanding of all the things that you have to pull together to run a business. In this assignment, you learned that every decision was a financial decision that had to have a payoff for the shareholders.

CEO Don Fites notes,

> I came back here as vice president of the product control group, as it was called in those days. We ran new product development programs, all corporate scheduling of product, all worldwide pricing, and worldwide sourcing. I knew from that experience that there must be a better way of running the company.

It is one thing to talk about the pros and cons of centralization and decentralization from a theoretical or academic point of view. It is quite another to live through the experience. Since many of the senior managers at Caterpillar had served time in the product control group, they knew it was not the right way to be organized. Each thought there must be a better way of running the company.

The Reorganization

Caterpillar is currently organized into 17 profit center divisions and 5 support service divisions. The current organization is virtually the same as the organization that was created in 1990 (14 profit center divisions and 4 service center divisions). Don Fites explains,

> I became the CEO of the company in 1990 at about the time we decided that we needed to restructure the company.
>
> The company was way too functionally organized, and we spent most of our time communicating with each other as opposed to communicating with the real world. The decision-making process was too concentrated, and I lived through enough of that to understand what sort of inefficiencies that created. So we had a lot of consultants in and spent an awful lot of time talking about this even before I became chairman.
>
> Eventually, in early 1990, I sat down here one day and laid out an organization chart, which I still have here in my desk. It's pretty much the way we are still organized today. The key to this organization is our division vice presidents, who sort of run their own companies. They have their own profit and loss statements, their own balance sheets, their own accountabilities and responsibilities. In the executive office, I have four group presidents who have five or six vice presidents reporting to them. During the entire reorganization process, there was no question in my mind of the atmosphere I wanted. The question in my mind was, "How do I reorganize to make it work?"
>
> Having been a company of essentially functional specialists, having been that way since our inception in 1925, we have changed the entire concept, the entire culture of the company. It was done through the accounting system and the compensation system that followed.

In our experiences at many other companies, we have not found another CEO who credits his accounting group with playing such an instrumental role in changing the culture of the entire firm. After describing some of the essential features of the new decentralized organization, we will take a closer look at the role the corporate accounting group played in the reorganization.

The Accountable System

Caterpillar's corporate accountability system is built around customers (the marketing division), products (the product divisions), and support services (the service divisions). Each business unit is responsible for understanding all aspects of that business and the unique characteristics of that business and then developing strategies to improve that business. In the new organization, the product managers are responsible for integrating all of the necessary functions under the product umbrella. The old functional organization was eliminated, and the functional specialists were dispersed throughout the product organizations.

The accountable system represented an entirely new way of looking at the world to the managers who had lived through the previous functional organization. Al Rassi, Vice President, explains,

> One of the excitements of the new organization is having a P&L. We know the elements of the profit and know where we can go in and put pressure on to improve the profit.

> It is a night-and-day difference to manage a cost center versus a profit center. In a cost center, the only place you could concentrate on was the cost side. Now we can concentrate on where we buy our materials, components, and services.

Jim Owens, Group President, adds,

> We have always had a good cost system, but we also had a cost problem. We have gotten out of some businesses based on the discipline of accountable profit. Each manager has to decide on how to make his accountable profit. You are encouraged to get price realization. Market-based transfer pricing has driven the system. ROA has had a big impact on capital spending. In addition to closing some facilities, we stopped building new ones. We also have had a major impact on inventories, somewhat less of an impact on receivables.

Don Fites notes,

> In looking back at that process, the thing that drives this organization and drives the success we have experienced is the accountable profit system that we set up. There is no duplication of profit. You only count profit once. Everybody has their own balance sheet and gets charged for their assets based on a blend of debt and equity.

> The system has done exactly what we wanted it to do in terms of changing the culture, making people bottom-line oriented, making people action oriented, making them understand the consequences of their actions.

Ron Bonati, Vice President, says,

> Pre-reorganization, we did not have anybody focused on specific businesses. We just focused on the business in total. With the reorganization, we started cutting it up. It's amazing the kind of focus you can get when you cut it up and make people accountable for the pieces.

Now when we judge business initiatives, our executive office can ask us what kind of profits we can make, what capital expenditures we might need to make, all tied to a special business. Heretofore, before the reorganization, we would have swept it up into a big pile. There wasn't a focus group responsible for it.

[Under the accountable profit system], I know what I am responsible for. I know what the rules are. I know how the accounting goes. I know what the financial implications are. I know what I have said I am going to do, and I know they are going to measure me on what I have said I am going to do. I'm going to get that day in court, and I am going to get to show those same charts a year from now that I showed December 23 [1996]. Here's what I said I was going to do, and here's what I did.

Measurement and Accountability

All of the senior managers we interviewed attributed the success of the reorganization and the new accountable profit system to the speed with which the new system was put in place. Don Fites explains,

I think the whole secret of making this thing work as well or as fast or as broadly as it did was the sort of brain power that went into setting up these measuring systems and flowing out of that, the compensation systems. Although there were a lot of other people involved in the process, the accounting people really drove the change.

We were able to change the entire culture of this company through the development of a new financial reporting system. We developed the new system over a period of a few months. There was no other way it could have been done.

I remember it was about May 1990 that I told the accounting-led team that I wanted this financial reporting system in place so we could budget for our new organization in 1991. I wanted every one of the divisions to have their own financial systems, P&Ls, balance sheets, and transfer prices.

The team said it was impossible. I said do it.

So not only did they do it, I do not know of any system today that is as good as the one we have. We have only made minor adjustments to the system since we put it in place six years ago.

When it comes to performance, Ron Bonati has a nice way of linking the organization to the measurement system. He says, "You know, 'if you're not keeping score, you're just practicing.' We evaluate all of our managers based on the hard numbers. No one questions the numbers anymore. I know how well my dealer and my people have performed each month."

As a member of the original, interdisciplinary, ad hoc team created by Don Fites to conceptualize the measurement system, Lou Jones helped chart the course for the movement from cost centers to profit centers and support service centers. He explains,

> The rules were very simple. There had to be accountability for decisions at the core of the new measurement process. "Allocations" was a word we were no longer going to use. There were not going to be any allocations. The measurement process and measurement system had to have accountability for decisions at the core.

> We did not want a profit center to review its results and say to our executive office, "Gee, we would have achieved our financial goals had it not been for the corporate allocations you made us take." Nothing will kill the effectiveness of a financial measurement quicker than allocations!

> We had to ask and answer two questions in designing the system. First, what would happen in the real world, and what would happen if everyone had to act as independent parties? Second, what type of behavior is the measurement system going to drive? When the reorganization was announced, there was no system in place that measured the complete value chain of the business.

> In designing the new measurement system, (1) accountability had to be at the core, (2) the system had to include a return-on-asset target, (3) we had to make sure that we were driving good business behavior, consistent with what would happen in the real world, and (4) we would need to use market-based transfer prices for product, component, and part transfers between profit centers, due to the integrated structure of our company.

Based on our interviews, there is no question that managers at Caterpillar know what they are held accountable for, know the ROA targets they have to hit, and know how to get results. When they talk about the accountable profit system, two topics always come to the forefront: transfer prices and ROA.

Transfer Prices

If you want to hold managers accountable for profit, you had better be able to measure profitability. If managers are going to be held accountable for the bottom line, they had better have responsibility for all of the elements that contribute to the bottom line—sales, costs, and capital. Doug Oberhelman, CFO, says,

> Our cost system is second to none. Recently we put a feature into our system that shows the profitability of a machine wherever it is built in the world. We can roll up the cost on a worldwide basis. I think our accounting group is absolutely the best in class. Out of the six divisions that report to me (Accounting, Information Technology, Industrial Relations, Treasury, the Marketing support group, and Tax), Accounting gets the highest employee ratings.

In all of the interviews we conducted with nonfinancial managers, no one questioned the integrity of Caterpillar's cost management system. In a cost-center environment, everyone focused on costs. Cost information was not the problem with the decentralization of the company. The problem was how to transfer products between divisions in this highly integrated company. In order to hold people accountable for the bottom line, you need to have a top line for sales. The ad hoc measurement committee decided to use market-based transfer prices to establish accountability for the intracompany sales. Don Fites says,

> Transfer pricing is driving the right behavior in the sense of helping us focus on what we should be driving out of the company. What this is doing, is driving things out of the company that we are not good at. It's also validating that we are very good at a lot of things in terms of cutting iron, welding iron, bending iron, designing products, designing engines, or running computer-based systems. Jim Despain [Vice President of the Track-Type Tractors Division] does not have to buy his products and services internally. He does not have to buy anything internally. All we need to know from Jim is what he sold and how much money we made from his operations. What this [transfer-pricing system] does is drive market reality into all facets of the business.

Lou Jones notes,

> Since every manager was to be held accountable for their own bottom line, they had to become intelligent purchasers and sellers. Under the old system, transfers were made at cost, and, although costs were important, there was no accountability for bottom-line results. Cost centers were measured against plan, not bottom-line profit. With P&L responsibility, profit centers knew they were being judged on the bottom line, and no one was willing to eat someone else's cost problem.

If it cost $100 to make a product and the market price is $75, and I expect to do business with you, I have to transfer it to you at $75. In that way, I cannot pass my cost problem on to your financial statements. So the behavior we are trying to drive is to pinpoint where the cost problems are and have the right people address them.

According to Gary Stroup, "The one single catalyst that has helped the components division go from losing an awful lot of money in 1992 to making a very nice profit in 1996 is the pressure of transfer pricing and bottom-line P&L responsibility."

As Ron Bonati notes,

Everyone trusts the numbers in the system. We do now. It was painful and difficult in the beginning, but now it works. Everything on my financial statement is mine. I've imposed it on myself. For all service department charges, I know what I'm charged, and I agreed to it. It's now six years, and everyone understands the ground rules. All transfer price negotiations are based on the marketplace. Everyone has to justify their position on transfer prices.

Jim Owens adds,

Our system of accountable profit and measurement has given people pieces of the business with line-of-sight objectives. Our accountable financial statements ultimately have to reconcile to our legal entity reporting that we include in the annual report. This system was key to the whole reorganization. It provided the discipline of the market and helped managers shine some light on their cost problems.

One additional benefit that Caterpillar has derived from the bottom-line P&L focus involves the political climate within the company. Doug Oberhelman says, "There is very little interdepartmental politics anymore because of the P&L focus. The other [cost center] model just produced blame."

Return on Assets

If the concept of accountable profit helped managers develop a line of sight on the bottom line, ROA helped them focus on the assets (or capital) under their control. The importance of the ROA-based measurement system was voiced by managers at all levels within the organization. Don Fites says,

Well, I think that the keys to a good measurement system are: Do people understand it? Do they have a line of sight? Do they understand how they can impact their future? Do they understand how they can affect their incentive compensation or their performance?

Al Rassi, Vice President, adds,

ROA is so simple, even I understand it. That's sort of the test I put to things. In the good old dictionary formula, there are only two ways you can change ROA. You can either put more on the top, or you put less on the bottom. Anyway, assets are something pretty simple. ROA works well here; even engineers understand assets. They understand costs, they understand prices, and they understand ROA.

ROA is a big part of what we do. ROA is our driving force. We do very little here that does not have a positive influence on ROA. On our new product development program, we have an affordability limit on capital spending and research and engineering (R&E).

You decide what you can afford to spend next year when you take your sales, your product mix, and your profits into account. Once you know what your profits are going to be, you crank in what you can afford to spend on capital and R&E, then determine its effect on return on assets.

We use DCF [discounted cash flow] to look at the economics of a project. We then run the numbers through our affordability index. We may come to the conclusion that we will take a hit on ROA if it is a good investment for the future. We are judged against a target ROA for our division and within the context of hitting an overall 15 percent corporate ROA.

Jim Cromer, Business Manager, notes,

If I were you [the interviewers], the next question I would ask is, "Why don't you take ROA down to each of your product groups?" And the answer is—we do have a product manager business statement that breaks down our overall business into product groups, and the product groups use that information to help manage their worldwide businesses.

One thing we do not do is to use that lower tier information for incentive compensation purposes. Because of the interrelationships between product groups, we keep our incentive compensation at the division level. This concept may change in the future, but for the present, it allows us to make very effective utilization of our shared resources. In addition, the movement of people between product groups is a significant benefit to all product groups.

Throughout the interview process, managers talked at length about measuring performance in terms of ROA. To our minds, everyone was well aware of the strengths and weaknesses of using ROA or any other performance metric in running the business.[5] For Caterpillar, one of the real benefits of evaluating the profit centers in terms of ROA was getting its capital expenditure program under control.

Capital Expenditures

In Caterpillar's highly centralized, functional organization, assets were owned at the corporate level, not at the business-unit level. In a very real sense, capital was a "free" good. If managers were only being evaluated against their cost center budget, why should they be concerned about capital? Get as much as you can as often as you can and live within your cost budget. Doug Oberhelman says,

> For the last several years until last year, we did not encourage people to talk about growth. We had a serious situation on our hands. Costs out of control, we were in some of the wrong businesses, we weren't focused, we had little emphasis on asset turnover. For so long, we just abused assets in this company. The powers that be said that we needed a measurement to not only increase the bottom line, but also decrease assets. We had to start to focus on two things [earnings and assets] rather than just one [earnings].

Bob Gallagher, Corporate Controller, adds,

> When we created the measurement system, we coined the terms "accountable profit" and "accountable assets." We said to each profit center team that these are the assets you are accountable for, and in fact we are going to charge you interest on those assets. We are going to charge you 4 percent on the baseline assets and the going rate (9 percent) for incremental assets. When they add assets, they get a double whammy because they get a capital charge and the assets go into their base. Anyone reducing assets gets a 9 percent credit. If you bring inventories down, you get a 9 percent credit on beginning-of-the-year balances.

> The measurement system has done wonders for what other people saw as a giant flaw under the old system, where people saw capital as being free. In some years, we were spending 10 percent of sales on capital expenditures. There were no reservations, few restrictions, on capital. You go after as much as you can get. In the past, every plant manager wanted a high-rise warehouse. Now they are tearing them down.

Gary Stroup notes,

> About the time all of the bugs were worked out of the measurement system, we [the components division] were ready for fine-tuning. Early on, it was "stop the bleeding," and we didn't need good measurements then because it did not take a rocket scientist to figure out what was going on.

> In 1991, we spent $103 million on capital. In the next year, we dropped it to $56 million versus the plan to take it up to $120 million. We took that $56 million down to $44 million and then took that $44 million down to $40 million.

> Today, we have more sales than we did five and one-half years ago. We have held our prices fairly flat through that entire five-and-a-half-year period and are using less capital and fewer people today than we did then. That's the difference between being a profit center and a cost center. Capital and people became luxuries, not necessities.

Taking Stock

The changes described up to this point take us to the early 1990s. By then, Caterpillar was using ROA to link the new organization to the new measurement system. To make sure everyone was starting to develop a market orientation in this highly integrated company, intracompany sales were recorded at market-based transfer prices. Every product manager was now being held accountable for his or her own profits and assets.

If we had conducted the management interviews at the end of this period, we would not have been able to talk about Caterpillar's incentive compensation system and other workforce initiatives. These changes were still to come.

Once Caterpillar got the right organization and the right measurement system in place and began to use ROA as the primary performance measure, it was time to get the workforce more involved. The first workforce initiative was to build a basic level of business competency among the division vice presidents, the product line managers, and members of the business-unit teams. The second initiative was to put an incentive compensation system in place that was compatible with the new performance measurement system.

Business Competency

Wouldn't it be nice if every company could reorganize its business practices, develop a new measurement system, and have all of the employees come to work on Monday without any training? Think of the costs the company could avoid if everyone knew how to translate the CEO's vision for the future into a current reality.

Since the corporate accounting group had the primary responsibility for designing the new measurement system, the responsibility for training fell to that same group. Corporate accounting saw the need to be proactive in developing the training needed to ensure the success of the new measurement system. Don Fites explains,

> Corporate accounting is really corporate consulting. They help this company become more successful by helping other people focus on the right things. In their own way, they are entrepreneurs. They're causing the company to act and respond appropriately to the external environment out there.

> I must say that corporate accounting developed some really good training programs over the last several years. Lou [Jones] and his people came up with all kinds of business games [the accountability game, the accounting game, the cash flow game, and the cost connection] to bring our managers up to speed.

According to Lou Jones, all the business games were based on "accelerated learning" principles. With a new organization and a new measurement system, people had to come up to speed fast. The type of training that appealed to the creative right brain of people became the model for all programs. According to Lilli Davis, Cost Methodology and Reporting Manager,

> The accountability game classes were a response to the need for everyone to understand the reorganization and how the new performance system worked. About 8,000 management and salaried people have gone through this program.

> The team that developed the performance measurements also developed the accountability game. Then we built our training programs on their very right-brain approach to training, very visual, very colorful. Other games are the accounting game, the cash flow game, and the cost connection.

> A group in Treasury created the currency game based on the same principles we used to develop our games. This game helps people understand the impacts of currency on the business.

As discussed more fully below, saying that corporate accounting is really corporate consulting extends beyond the games that have been developed to build business competency. Corporate accounting provides a wide variety of services to the business units and services that must be paid for by the business units. In the context of Caterpillar's overall transformation, the transformation of the corporate accounting group would become more evident after the incentive compensation system was put in place.

Incentive Compensation

Senior management did not stop when it linked the organization to the measurement system through the ROA concept. After getting people up to speed on how the new accountability system worked, management took the additional step of linking the workforce to the organization through the incentive compensation system. It is one thing to measure performance in terms of ROA. It is quite another thing to reward individuals for achieving or exceeding their ROA targets.

At Caterpillar, every manager's compensation is tied, at least in part, to how well their business and the corporation performs against its business plan. Don Fites explains, "The incentive system goes all the way down throughout the organization. It is incentive based on performance better than plan, not a bonus."

Lou Jones continues,

> The incentive compensation for a typical product manager in a profit center might be weighted in the following manner: corporate ROA, 25 percent; division ROA, 50 percent; and 25 percent on achieving prespecified critical success factors.

> The incentive compensation for managers in a service center like corporate accounting would be weighted in the following manner: corporate ROA, 50 percent; 30 percent on the ROA performance of a market basket of internal customers; and 20 percent on internal process improvement initiatives. We have 17 different initiatives for the current year that fit into that last 20 percent. These initiatives create a direct line of sight for all of our people. Everyone knows just where and how they are contributing to the achievement of our corporate accounting targets.

Mark Thompson, Business Analysis Manager, says,

> The incentive system drives the right behavior. It does not really matter how much of a percentage you put on it. If you put 1 percent on it, people

work toward that. And it's not so much the money. There is a lot of peer pressure on not wanting to let any of the team members down.

With incentive compensation, we have the ability to drive the right behavior. I think that is probably the reason we went to incentive compensation. With the profit sharing, your payout was not tied to your performance. Under incentive compensation, it is how well we do versus the plan. Each one of the critical success factors—each one—has an impact. It's not boom or bust. It's always trying to drive the right behavior year after year after year through things we can do to improve the company.

Given the importance of the business-unit profitability and the division and corporate ROA, financial information is more widely shared in Caterpillar today than it ever was in the past. Open-book management is driving improved business results.

Workforce Initiatives

As change after change unfolded within the company, it became increasingly obvious that the limits of technology, organization, measurement, and incentive were being reached. These changes had a dramatic and positive effect on Caterpillar. However, these changes were initiated from above. They did not bubble up from the bottom of the organization. As it turns out, it was only a matter of time before the emphasis on people was intensified.

Besides providing financial incentives tied to performance, the only thing left to do was get the workforce more involved. Al Rassi explains,

> About 1993, we realized that we needed to add something to our business strategy on values. East Peoria took the lead, adding common values to their mission and vision statement. Several of our innovative people went off site (with the business development group from corporate accounting) to develop a set of values that describes to all of our employees and the outside world who we are and how we intend to do business. The bottom line on our values was to make Aurora a great place to work, where people look forward to coming to work on Monday as they do to going home on Friday.

Jim Despain, Vice President, says,

> I was trained to be authoritative. I did not trust anybody. We were trained not to trust anybody. It was part of the culture. In the 1980s, we were considered one of the best managed companies in America, and we did not trust each other. So what does that tell you?

We've got to trust each other. We've got to respect each other. We had problems of trust with the unions, the first shift with the second shift, the second with the third, office with the shop, shop with the office, one layer of management with another layer of management—it was an adversarial culture. So trusting each other, respecting each other, became a high priority. We used outside consultants as a reality check. We used outside people for facilitation, but the programs we developed were of our own making.

At each of the sites that we visited, other Caterpillar vice presidents were trying to incorporate some form of common-values objectives into their mission statements. Corporate Accounting Services calls the emphasis on people its people statement:

Corporate Accounting Services People Statement

We believe people should be able to work in an environment where all are shown respect, given responsibility, and are trusted to perform meaningful, enriching work with the support and encouragement of others.

☐ Respect—People are treated with consideration, dignity, and regarded as honored and valued fellow employees.

☐ Responsibility—People understand the importance of their role and are accountable for the results they produce.

☐ Trust—People have the integrity that enables fellow employees and customers to rely on them and have confidence in the results.

☐ Meaningful, Enriching Work—Jobs add value in meeting the needs of our customers while providing the opportunity for an enriched work experience for the individual.

☐ Support and Encouragement—People support one another in the pursuit of meeting customer needs and those of the individual.

Although the emphasis on people at Caterpillar is important, even more important in terms of our research is that people from corporate accounting are helping the business units develop their mission statements and business strategies.

We conclude the Caterpillar story by focusing on the support service sides of the business. As one of Caterpillar's support service divisions, the financial organization is required to recover all of its costs (other than some "exempt" service charges) from fees paid by the business units that use these services.

In a sense, Caterpillar has come full circle. The corporate accounting group within the financial organization that developed the new performance measurement system has to follow the same rules as everybody else. If they cannot convince customers that their services are worth buying, they will have a cost problem that has to be eliminated. However, as we shall see, corporate accounting has converted a potential cost problem into a service opportunity.

Support Services, the Financial Organization

Up to this point in the Caterpillar story, the 17 profit centers created in the reorganization have received the bulk of our attention. The vice presidents who run these profit centers all have a line of sight to the bottom line and know that their performance will be judged against the target ROA negotiated with the executive office. But what about the service centers and the vice presidents who run them? How do they fit into Caterpillar's overall management operating philosophy? Don Fites notes,

> There are also five service center divisions, which were essentially old general office functions. They all became cost centers with a sunset clause every year. They have to recover all of their costs. They have to sell all of their costs to someone every year. They cannot lose money. They have to break even. They became providers of service to the profit center divisions.

Jim Owens, Group President, says,

> I became the CFO in 1992 and was in that job for about two years before becoming a group vice president three years ago. The CFO is responsible for managing our Corporate Services Division. Corporate Services provides consulting services to profit center divisions based on their particular functional expertise. Prior to taking the CFO position, I was president of Solar Turbines, our wholly owned gas turbine subsidiary in San Diego.
>
> In a 1992 employee survey, over 80 percent of the people said they would recommend Solar as a place to work, and Solar employees were paid at the prevailing market rate. In the Corporate Services Division, just over 50 percent of our employees said they would recommend Caterpillar as a place to work in 1993, and many people in the division had salaries well above the prevailing market rate. These staff functions used to be holders of the reins, controllers of the ship. All of a sudden, they became a service division

when the chairman was trumpeting customer focus and bottom-line results in the profit centers. We had a terrible morale problem.

They had little idea how our total business worked. They didn't know customers or what customer service meant. It took some time for them to start thinking of themselves as having an expertise that the businesses needed and that they had to sell their services to the business units that needed that expertise. It also took a while for them to realize that the business units could go elsewhere to buy the services they needed.

So we put more line-of-sight objectives into their compensation packages: 25 percent of their incentive compensation was based on the corporate ROA, 60 percent was based on the ROA of a market basket of the customers they served, and 15 percent was based on meeting a challenging set of objectives based on achieving their critical success factors. It worked. They're now thinking like business people and meeting their customer's expectations. Morale in the service divisions has improved significantly.

To a certain extent, converting the old "controllers of the ship" into service providers is like sentencing a prosecuting attorney to a prison where the inmates had all been convicted by that attorney. To make matters worse, the profit centers did not have to purchase the services offered by the corporate services group. They could (and many did) go outside of Caterpillar and buy the services they needed on the open market. It is not hard to understand that there would be a morale problem in corporate services.

Our interviews with managers working in the corporate services area indicated that the decision to put support services people on the incentive compensation system went a long way toward reducing the stigma associated with playing a supporting role. The incentive compensation program was extended to include the support service organizations two years after incentive compensation was introduced into the profit centers.

Currently, all support service costs have to be recovered through charges to the business units. Only a small amount of costs are "exempt" from Caterpillar's market-driven philosophy. Don Fites explains,

The only caveat to all this [support service concept] is that there is about $130 million (1/2 percent of sales) worth of expenses that are exempt, and the single largest item in those is about $35 million in research, which I sponsor and which is not yet finite enough to be assigned to a particular product or a particular service. That, plus I pay for some corporate accounting, treasury, tax, and some legal—the compliance stuff. But those things have a sunset budget. They have to justify the money they are spending on these functions every year.

Every other expense in the company is market driven, and it is up to the purchaser to buy the other services from these support divisions. The five service divisions have to sell their services or eliminate them.

With respect to the corporate accounting group, the people who developed the performance measurement system were now going to be subject to the discipline of the market. If they could not recover their costs through charges to the business units, they would have to downsize the group. Doug Oberhelman says,

The demand for most services comes from the business groups. In accounting, we formed a small group to do business consulting. We went into that with the idea that we would only expand if there was demand for which people would pay (internal customers and Caterpillar dealers who will send us real cash). Our distributors do not have to go to us. They can go to McKinsey, Andersen Consulting, etc. It is an absolute litmus test. It is a wonderful thing to watch and see your people respond to the challenge.

In addition to corporate accounting, corporate information services, corporate tax, corporate treasury, investor relations, and marketing support services report to the CFO. The managers of each of these services know that they have only two ways of increasing headcount and increasing their budgets: either convince the CEO to approve an increase in expenditures on "exempt" services (a most unpleasant task to say the least), or provide services demanded by the profit centers at a level of price and quality that the outside cannot beat.

Within the corporate controller's operations (corporate accounting services), the accounting "growth engine" is located within Cost Management and Business Services. Cost Management and Business Services is made up of two groups—Cost Management and Business Analysis Services, and Business Development Services. The managers of each of these groups are responsible for "growing their own businesses" by selling services to the profit centers.

What captured our attention in talking to the managers of these groups and the project managers working within each group was their clear "market" focus. Both groups have developed their own internal consulting brochures that describe and explain the services they offer. They also provide a list of the clients who have used their services.

For example, the Cost Management and New Venture Services group identifies itself as a Division of Caterpillar Corporate Accounting Services. The services the group provides include

☐ Business Analysis

☐ Venture Analysis

☐ Competitive Analysis

☐ Cost Methodology and Reporting

☐ Product Cost Systems

☐ New Venture Financial Implementation Support Team (NVFIST)

The description of NVFIST included in the promotional brochure follows:

> This support team brings together the combined expertise of accounting, treasury, and tax to provide financial project management and dedicated resources to new companies during their start-up phase. In addition to preparing a detailed financial implementation plan, we will assist local management in developing their business processes and reporting routines by
>
> ☐ Researching local business practices and reporting requirements
>
> ☐ Making recommendations for local accounting policies, including depreciation, inventory valuation, and absorption and funding/treasury issues
>
> ☐ Structuring the chart of accounts
>
> ☐ Identifying adjustments needed to convert local statements to a U.S. GAAP basis
>
> ☐ Helping in the selection of financial software

Current clients include ventures in China, Russia, England, and Italy.

Not to be outdone, Business Development Services markets its services as follows:

> **What Is Business Development Services?**
>
> Business Development Services is Caterpillar's consulting group formed in 1991 to provide consulting services to the profit and service centers, executive office, dealers, and suppliers. We advise our customers' top management on issues of strategy, process improvement, benchmarking, market assessments and acquisitions. We help our customers resolve internal business issues, anticipate and respond to external threats and opportunities, and make substantial and lasting improvements in their performance.

What Is Our Mission?

We are dedicated to positively impacting our customers' strategic direction and business performance.

The brochure also identifies recent customer engagements and explains each of the group's services in more detail.

Tim Cunningham describes the evolution of Business Development Services:

We learned how to do the business-strategy consulting by working with outside consultants. We then decided that we could offer those same services on an in-house consulting basis. This was about 15 months after the company reorganized into business units. We started to get a lot of interest in what we were doing from the service divisions who were trying to figure out their roles in this new organization. We helped them develop a strategy based on what they saw their role in the new organization to be.

In mid-1991, Bob Gallagher saw us as a fit with corporate accounting services. Just five years ago, four of us came over from data processing, joined by one accountant, to start this new group. We now have 17 people in our group and are looking to add some additional expertise from outside of Caterpillar.

As we have seen, the financial organization has played an important role in the transformation of the company over the last decade and a half.

Summing Up

In telling the Caterpillar story, we have not focused on the market and have hardly mentioned the creation of shareholder value. Given Caterpillar's focus on ROA and market-based transfer pricing, managers know who their customers are, they know who their suppliers are, and they know they do not have to buy any corporate services if they do not want to. To a large extent, a product market mentality has been internalized at Caterpillar. But what about the capital markets? What about shareholders?

We leave you with the CEO's thoughts about creating shareholder value:

I look at shareholder value as not something that our people have to understand. That's my objective and the objective of the group presidents on this floor.

There are only a couple of ways to increase shareholder value. You can increase the price of the shares or increase the dividend. I prefer to do a bit of both, quite frankly, but believe the preferable way is to increase the value of the shares. Increasing the value of the shares fits right in with what I want to do, and that is grow the company.

I am convinced that if you put the right tools in place—the right measurement tools—and you put the right incentives in place, the job that I have now is not sitting here beating my brains out trying to decide how to grow the company. My job is to select the best 10 out of the 30 or 40 proposals that these divisions are coming up with almost every year—major proposals as to how they want to grow their business.

We are overrun with proposals. We are throwing off over $1 billion in free cash flow a year. We can finance a hell of a lot of things. When we sit down and take our annual strategic look at the company, the question is not how we are going to grow. The question is, "Which one of these growth opportunities that is being put forth by our divisions are we going to finance, and which of these divisions are we going to hold where they are or hold to slower growth or put some constraints on in terms of their spending? Which proposals will generate the most shareholder value in the medium and long term?"

So that process is working because we selected the right measurement system to motivate people and to help people understand their business. We are turning loose the creative juices of seven or eight thousand people who are trying to grow their businesses as opposed to seven or eight people up here in our executive offices on the seventh floor.

For Caterpillar, if you put the right pieces in place, you can put the puzzle together. And if you are a financial person working at Caterpillar, you are expected to play a major role in putting the pieces together.

People Interviewed

Executive Office

Don Fites
Chief Executive Officer

Glenn Barton
Group President—Executive Office

Jim Owens
Group President—Executive Office

Corporate Services Division

Doug Oberhelman
Vice President and CFO

Treasury

Lynn McPheeters
Corporate Treasurer

Corporate Accounting

Bob Gallagher
Corporate Controller

Brad Halverson
Manager—Financial Accounting Services

Barb Hodel
No Error, On Demand Champion

Lou Jones
Manager—Cost Management and Business Services

Marylean Abney
Manager—Cost Management and New Venture Services

Lilli Davis
Manager—Cost Methodology and Reporting

Gary Decker
Manager—New Venture Development

Tim Cunningham
Business Development Services

Wheel Loaders and Excavators Division

Al Rassi
Vice President

Bob Meng
Product Manager—Medium Wheel Loaders

Jim Cromer
Business Manager

Mark Thompson
Business Analysis Manager

Track-Type Tractors Division

Jim Despain
Vice President and General Manager

Ken Zika
Business Manager

Parts and Service Support Division

Jim Baldwin
Vice President

Medium Engines

Dan Murphy
Vice President

Component Products Division

Gary Stroup
Vice President

North American Commercial Division

Ron Bonati
Vice President

Endnotes

1. *Changing Roles of Financial Management: Getting Close to the Business*, Financial Executives Research Foundation, 1990.

2. The corporate accounting group performed the competitor analysis study that documented the 30 percent cost problem. As Lou Jones, Cost Management and Business Services Manager, mentioned to us, "We did 'competitive benchmarking' before the term was invented. We just called it competitor analysis."

3. Lou's brief history of Caterpillar also included the reorganization of marketing in 1983 and the revision of the new product introduction process in 1989. These events were not identified as being that important in understanding how the financial organization contributions fit into management's overall operating philosophy.

4. When Caterpillar first reorganized, 14 profit center divisions and 4 service divisions were created. The current organization consists of 17 profit center divisions and 5 service divisions.

5. Since talk about economic valued added is currently making the rounds in the business community, several managers at Caterpillar (and each of the other companies included in the study) would take some time to describe why they were not using economic valued added. Since no firm in the study was using economic valued added, we see no reason to make more than a passing reference to this topic.

3

Nucor Corp.

When we ask managers in executive education programs if they know much about Nucor, we get mixed responses. Managers from firms who do business with Nucor or compete against Nucor have nothing but praise for the company. Nucor is considered a fierce competitor in the steel and steel products businesses. Other managers who have heard the Nucor name but are not directly involved with the steel business typically respond by asking a question that goes something like this: "Isn't Nucor that little steel company that built a minimill that allows them to compete against the Japanese? I think I remember reading something about them 15 or 20 years ago."

What they recall is the publicity surrounding that first steel mill that Nucor built in 1969 when Ken Iverson and Sam Siegel played "bet the company" by borrowing $6 million from Wachovia bank to build that first minimill. Since that time, Nucor has built quite a few more minimills. And, by the way, Nucor is now the number two steelmaker in the United States with plans to become number one by the year 2000.

To a certain extent, we could tell the Nucor story in terms of the revolution that occurred when Ken Iverson was named President and Sam Siegel was named Financial Vice President of a company on the verge of bankruptcy in 1965. By 1972, the company had changed so much that management adopted a new name, "Nucor." Prior to 1972, it was known as the Nuclear Corporation of America, a company involved in nuclear instrumentation, electronics, and the steel joist businesses.

In 1965, the electronics business was sold off and the company was rebuilt around the steel joist business, operating under the Vulcraft name. By 1969, the company had built its first steel mill to provide its two Vulcraft divisions with high-quality, low-cost steel. The name change reflected the fact that management was directing all of its energies toward the steel joist business and the steelmaking business.[1] The story of Nucor's entry into the steelmaking business has been told in a very

60

entertaining manner by Richard Preston,[2] and we will not attempt to repeat his fine work here.

Because we will not be focusing on the management revolution that occurred at Nucor, we could focus on how the company has evolved from that revolutionary beginning in 1965. However, telling the Nucor story in that fashion would be like saying that *Moby Dick* was a story about a whale. The facts would all be there, but the story would be devoid of life.

The story that we will be telling is about a company where business strategy is tied directly to a people-oriented corporate culture. In the Nucor system, employee compensation and job security are directly linked to productivity. The Nucor organization (with only four layers of management) and the measurement system (emphasizing tons of steel produced, earnings, ROA, and ROE) support the overall business strategy and employee-oriented corporate culture. However, the organizational structure and the measurement system do not play a dominant role in the Nucor system.

In the words of Dan DiMicco, Vice President and General Manager of the Nucor-Yamato Steel jointly owned facility,

> It's the system, the system, the system. It's the people, the people, the people.

> The key to our success is people and good communications. If you want to define success, you go back to some basic core beliefs and principles. The key to the Nucor system is that you treat people the way you would like to be treated. We are treating people the way we would want to be treated, whether it's our personnel issues, our interpersonal issues, family issues, pay issues, benefit issues, or how I work with you. Treat people the way we wanted to be treated. That's what the Nucor system is all about—respect for people.

In terms of the conceptual model that was introduced in Chapter 1, the Nucor story may be visualized as shown in Figure 3.1.

In telling the Nucor story, we will cover all of the bases: the market, the workforce, the organization, and the measurement system. As we shall see,

1. Nucor's objective of growing the business by taking market share away from the competition sets the stage for all other aspects of Nucor's business strategy. To make that business strategy work,

FIGURE 3.1   Nucor: The Business Advocate Perspective—
Corporate Themes and Integrating Mechanisms

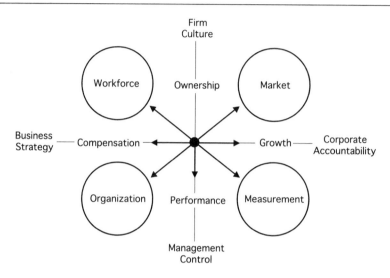

Nucor defines performance in terms of being the low-cost producer of high-quality steel in the United States.

2. What we will be referring to as the "Nucor system" is a manage-
    ment operating philosophy that rewards employees for their pro-
    ductivity. Nucor's incentive compensation system covers all
    employees and is tied directly to the performance of the people
    covered by one of four compensation plans. In addition to com-
    pensation, employee relations' principles at Nucor emphasize
    job security and fair treatment.

3. Everyone at Nucor is so integrated into the operations of their
    business units that it is hard to talk in terms of separate business
    functions having their own separate organizations (e.g., the fi-
    nancial organization, the human resource organization, the pro-
    curement organization). The only way to characterize Nucor's
    management operating style is to say that the company practices
    "lean administration." Being the low-cost producer of steel and
    steel products means being efficient in running all aspects of the
    business.

4. In a lean administrative environment, controllers (the corporate controller and the division controllers) are expected to be full participants in the business decision-making process. In this type of environment, accounting has to be the "no-brainer" part of their responsibilities

If readers are looking for a story that focuses on the unique role that the financial organization or financial people play in Nucor, they will probably be disappointed. Of all of the firms included in this study, Nucor has most fully integrated its financial aspects into the day-to-day operations of the business.

In telling the Nucor story, we will emphasize the following: (1) how the performance measurement system is tied directly to Nucor's overall business strategy; (2) how Nucor's incentive compensation system and employee relations program support the overall business strategy; and (3) how the financial organization supports open communications throughout the company.

Let the Story Begin

Business Strategy

The original decision to get into the steelmaking business was driven by the high cost and poor quality of the steel that Nucor's Vulcraft divisions were getting from the integrated steelmakers. With about 58 cents of every sales dollar tied to raw material costs, Nucor was not in control of the largest cost factor affecting net income. To get those costs under control, Ken Iverson decided to integrate backward and get into the steelmaking business. In 1968, Iverson and Sam Siegel negotiated a $6 million, 10-year loan to build their first steel mill. That $6 million loan represented the first and only time that Nucor played "bet the company."

The decision to get into the steelmaking business was a pragmatic one. If Nucor could produce steel for less than the prices being charged by the integrated steelmakers in the United States and the foreign competitors, Nucor could increase its profit margins in the steel joist business.

From those humble beginnings, Nucor has grown to be the number two steelmaker in America. In becoming the low-cost producer of steel in order to support its own steel joist business, Nucor set the stage for becoming the low-cost producer in the steel industry. Over the past 26 years, the ability to produce high-quality, low-cost steel has become Nucor's primary business strategy. John Correnti, President and CEO, explains,

> The total capacity of U.S. steel mills is only 93 million tons a year—17 million tons come from overseas. The idea is to drive down the cost of producing a ton of steel. Before Nucor got into the business, wide-flange beams were made by U.S. Steel, Bethlehem, Inland, and foreign steel makers. When high-rise buildings went up in America, 70 percent of the buildings were made from concrete and the other 30 percent were made from steel.

> You know why? Because they had the price of steel at $700 per ton. When we got into the business, we drove the price down to $260 per ton. U.S. Steel is gone. Inland is gone, and Bethlehem just announced that they are getting out of the business.

> Now the price is back up to $400 per ton. But guess what? Sixty-five percent of the buildings are made of steel and 35 percent are made of concrete. We made steel the material of choice vis-à-vis price. In the construction business, our competitors are wood and concrete, not the other steel companies. In automotive, it is plastics, aluminum, and composites. By driving costs down, you are improving your competitive advantage.

As discussed below, Nucor's continuing, short-term objective is to take market share away from the competition. However, Nucor's longer-term objective is to increase the total size of the steel business by making steel more attractive relative to concrete, plastics, aluminum, and composites. As John Correnti sees it, you accomplish both your short-run and long-run objectives through the same business strategy: being the low-cost producer. Terry Lisenby, Corporate Controller, says,

> Our business strategy is to take market share away from other producers. Steel is pretty much of a commodity, except for the upper end of steel products. It's price and service. Given equal service, it quickly becomes a price issue.

> The way to become the price leader, which we seem to be, is to be the low-cost producer. We have a simple pricing strategy. We price our products to run our mills flat out. We want the mills running at full capacity at all times. If our backlog starts to go down, we cut the price. We cut the price until the backlog reacts. If the backlog gets out too far, we raise the price.

Correnti adds,

> I can tell you next year how many tons of steel we are going to ship. I can't tell you what the margin is going to be on every ton. If we have a recession, we will drop the hell out of the price. Instead of making $40 to $50 a ton profit, we will only make a $10 profit.

> It's the basic law-of-the-jungle mentality: low cost, high quality wins at the end of the day, month, quarter, and the end of the year. It's the jungle mentality. It's survival of the fittest.

Dan DiMicco explains,

> Now we will keep our plants running seven days a week if that's what we can run them at, and we will lower the price if we have to [to] keep them running at capacity. We go after the market. If we are the lowest cost producer and we are taking care of our customers, we are going to be able to lower our price to the point where we are going to get the business and someone else is going to have cut back their workforce, or they are going to have to have layoffs, or they are going to have to go to a reduced workweek.

> It's survival of the fittest, and you had better be the fittest in this business. If you are not the fittest, you are not going to be around. It's pure and simple. Our system is definitely oriented to being the fittest.

According to Stewart Roberts, Division Controller,

> If the market is really poor, we are going to price our products to run at full capacity. Under our system, the production workers could be earning high bonuses while their divisions are just breaking even. The company emphasizes the production of the maximum tons of quality steel at the lowest possible cost.

At Nucor, everyone (executives, managers, and employees) knows the company's business strategy: take market share away from the competition by being the low-cost producer of quality steel. As the low-cost producer, you can cut your price and run your facilities at capacity. Profit margins may suffer at the bottom of the business cycle, but Nucor will not be the one to lose market share.

During the interview process at Nucor, it didn't matter if we were talking to financial managers or nonfinancial managers. Everyone was equally fluent in talking about the importance of growing the business by taking market share away from the competition. In a relatively flat total U.S. market for steel (110 million tons per year), everyone knows that the only way to grow your business is by cutting price when the market drops.

At Nucor, production is more important than price. In order to grow the business, you have to produce and sell more steel; and in order to sell more steel, you may have to cut the price to take market share away from the competition. As John Correnti said, he knows how much steel Nucor will produce next year; he just can't tell you what the margins are going to be. If a company is going to make money in a down market, it had better be a low-cost producer. And to be a low-cost producer, you had better be able to run your steel mills seven days a week.

In addition to being able to take market share away from the competition, being a low-cost producer has substantial benefits for the employees. In a down market when Nucor has to cut the price, the competition is going to have to cut back its workforce, have layoffs, or go to a reduced workweek before Nucor. Over the past 26 years, Nucor has had *no* layoffs. When the market has been at the lowest point in the business cycle, production has been cut back from seven to six, to five, to four, or even to three days a week, but everyone has had a job. The no-layoff policy is an important part of the Nucor employee relations program, second only to performance-based compensation.

Low-Cost Producer

The three critical internal financial measures that Nucor uses to run the business are (1) cost-per-ton of prime (high-quality) steel produced, (2) ROA, and (3) ROE.

Of the three measures, the cost-per-ton of steel produced is the most fundamental. If market share tells Nucor how well it is doing against the competition and Nucor is willing to cut price to increase market share, then the only way to be profitable is to control the cost-per-ton of steel produced. The profit margins are going to drop when the price is cut, but some profit will remain after the prices have been cut. Joe Stratman, Subsidiary Controller, says,

> Let's talk about cost. Scrap [raw material] is the largest cost, and that cost is driven by the market price for scrap. There is not much we can do about scrap. The next two costs are production driven—labor (man-hours per ton) and depreciation (absorbing capital). When employees produce the most quality tons that they can, then, whether it is on their minds or not, they are driving down the unit cost of the steel produced.

> If the equipment is down, they are not making bonus. Two-thirds to 80 percent of their pay is bonus. They know they have to maintain the equipment and keep it running as much as possible if they are going to get their bonus. They also want to maintain it the right way, so they do not want to destroy it. They do not want to kill the goose that lays the golden egg.

In order to keep the depreciation cost-per-ton to a minimum, the equipment must be run at or near full capacity; and to do that, the equipment has to be kept in good working order. If the equipment is down, you cannot produce any steel and employees cannot make their bonus. Now, making such statements is like promoting "apple pie and motherhood." In a perfect world, machines never break down, and they always run at full capacity. However, in a not-so-perfect world, machines break down and do not always run at full capacity.

In the Nucor system, the production groups (which include supervisors and maintenance people) keep the depreciation cost-per-ton down by keeping the equipment up and running at full capacity. They want to keep the equipment running at full capacity because two-thirds to 80 percent of their total compensation is based on a production bonus. The more tons of steel they produce above the target set for the machinery, the higher their bonus.

As several managers pointed out, the old "80/20" rule governs the people/technology equation at Nucor. Ken Iverson explains,

> Eighty percent of Nucor's success is based on people. The other 20 percent is based on the technology. Management provides the production workers with the technology, provides them with the economic incentives to use that technology to maximum advantage, and then gets out of the way.

People and Technology

One of the readings we assign to managers attending our executive education programs is *The Nucor Story*, the 16-page company brochure that explains Nucor's basic philosophy—to build steel manufacturing facilities economically and to operate them productively.[3] When asked to share their reactions to the Nucor story with the entire group, some managers will ask a question that goes something like this:

> Since weekly incentive compensation is based on exceeding production targets, how does management know that employees are not "sandbagging" to get the targets set as low as possible?

Before conducting our interviews at Nucor, we indicated that we would ask managers that question on the group's behalf. In their minds, something had to be wrong with a bonus plan that would allow employees to earn an average of 80 to 150 percent of the base wage.[4] As we discovered, nothing is wrong with the target-setting process at Nucor. The production targets and related bonuses are all part of the Nucor system. Iverson says,

> We set the target on roughly what the equipment will do in a normal environment, then we drop the target to 80 percent of that capacity. Then we adjust the target as we make more capital expenditures.

Sam Siegel, Vice Chairman and CFO, says,

> Targets are based on the good tonnage generated by the mills. The targets are set at 80 percent of the rated capacity as specified by the manufacturer.

John Correnti adds,

> [Target-setting is] easy. You buy the piece of machinery from the equipment supplier, say a caster, and you ask him how many tons per hour the equipment will do, say 100 tons per hour. So then we go to our employees and say the manufacturer said that this will do 100 tons per hour. So we set the base at 80 tons per hour. At 80 tons per hour you get $9 per hour, your base wage. For every ton an hour over that 80 tons, we are going to give you an extra 50 cents at the end of the week.
>
> So what they do is "Nucorize" the thing.

When we asked the vice presidents and controllers in the divisions and subsidiaries the same question, we got the same answer: Targets are set at 80 percent of capacity as specified by the manufacturer. Once the targets have been set, the production workers "Nucorize" the equipment. Employees have the freedom to change the equipment and change the production process to produce more tons of quality steel. However, if the change causes a shutdown, employees lose their bonus. At Nucor, the production employees do their own "risk/return" analysis. The analysis is not done by some "expert" far removed from the production floor.

If the first question managers in executive programs ask about Nucor has to do with "sandbagging," the second question has to do with maintenance:

> How does management make sure that the employees are not running the equipment into the ground by ignoring maintenance?

This is another good question that we said we would ask on the group's behalf. Ken Iverson responds,

> We are providing them [the production teams] with the equipment and the tools, and what we do is really put them in business for themselves. From 80 percent to 100 percent of capacity, they get a 25 percent bonus. So their incentive is to figure out how to get a "helluva" lot more bonus out of the equipment. They put on a bigger motor, or they run it faster, or they turn up the speed.

> I remember we had to straighten an angle, a one-by-one angle, and it is a laborious job. We bought this equipment that would produce the angle at 10 tons an hour based on industry standards. So we set the bonus at 8 tons an hour. Well, they kept turning it up to run at 20 tons an hour a year later. They did it all themselves. All you do is let them run it, give them the incentive, and let them go.

John Correnti says,

> We supply them with the technology, we supply them with the bricks and mortar, we supply them with the training, and then we put them in business for themselves. We put those 40 people in that one group in business for themselves. Our average pay was $58,000 per employee last year. We probably have the highest paid steel workers in the world. But guess what? We probably have the lowest labor cost to produce a ton of steel. It's not what you pay them, but what you pay them in relation to what they produce.

> The key to us is that little book right there [*The Nucor Story*]. Anybody can buy the technology. Technology is only 20 percent of the success equation.

> It's like you or me getting in the best race car. Are we going to win the race? Hell, no. It's the driver. It's the employees you put in the technology. You can't do it without the technology, but the technology does not assure you of anything. You have got to have the people.

Dan DiMicco adds, "It's the old '80/20' rule. You might say that it is 80 percent people and 20 percent technology."

As attested to from all of the interviews at Nucor, a company needs the latest technology, but once the technology is put into place, it's the people who are in the driver's seat. You get the productivity from the people, but people must have a reason to be concerned about productivity. That's where the incentive compensation system comes into play. Incentive compensation plays an important role in the Nucor culture.

The Nucor Culture: Incentive Compensation

Nucor describes its incentive compensation system as "performance-based compensation for goal-oriented people." *All* Nucor employees are covered by one of four basic compensation plans.

1. Production Incentive Plan—Employees working in production groups (averaging 20 to 40 employees) are paid weekly bonuses based on the production of their work group. Maintenance personnel and production supervisors are part of the bonus group and receive the same bonus as the employees they supervise. Incentive bonuses can average 80 percent to 150 percent of the base wage.

2. Department Manager Incentive Plan—Managers earn incentive bonuses paid annually based primarily on the ROA of their facility. These bonuses can be as much as 82 percent of base salary.

3. Non-Production and Non-Department Manager Incentive Plan—Participants include accountants, engineers, secretaries, clerks, receptionists, and a broad range of employee classifications. The bonus is based primarily on each ROA. This bonus can total 25 percent of salary.

4. Senior Officers Incentive Plan—Base salaries for senior officers are set below what executives receive in comparable companies (the 75th percentile of their peer group). A significant part of each senior officer's compensation is based on Nucor's return on stockholders' equity above a certain minimum earnings amount. If Nucor does well, the officer's compensation is well above average, as much as several times base salary. If Nucor does poorly, the officer's compensation is only the base salary and therefore, below the average pay for this type of responsibility.[5]

We will separate the discussion of Nucor's incentive compensation program into three parts: the production incentive plan, the ROA-based incentive plans for department heads and division staff personnel, and the senior officers' incentive plan. The key point to remember as we discuss each compensation plan is that the incentives have been designed to match the responsibilities of the employees and managers who are rewarded under the plan.

In discussing the plans, we will show how key operating and financial information is collected and monitored in support of each plan. The very existence of these incentive compensation plans promotes a culture of information sharing and open communications.

The Production Incentive Plan

The incentive compensation system reflects Nucor's management operating philosophy of putting people first—in particular, putting production people first. Ken Iverson explains,

> The company is built around groups. The first group is really the workers in the production incentive system. They are organized into groups that have bonuses that are linked to production and paid weekly. So when they really put out a great effort, they can see what they did because they get it back in money the next week.

According to John Correnti,

> In Nucor, the production employees are the kings and queens. That's the majority of our employees, and that's [who] we have all the programs benefiting first and foremost.

> They work in groups because an individual can't do it all. The production process is too interdependent. When you go into the plants, you will see it right in the locker rooms. If they work four crews, you will see it every day—crew A, crew B, crew C, crew D. Sunday, Monday, Tuesday, Wednesday, Thursday, Friday: tons, percent bonus; week-to-date, tons; week-to-date, percent bonus. So everybody knows where everybody stands.

> So not only is it a game, with a scorecard, not only who's making the most money. It's "We're 'A' crew."

Mike Parrish, Vice President and General Manager, adds,

> We are all in the same boat. We're a team. When two-thirds or more of our pay is based on how much we produce, do you think we are going to put up with someone who is not carrying their load? We are going to get in your face and tell you to do your work or get out of here. The system is almost self-policing.

The production incentive plan has been around since the Ken Iverson/ Sam Siegel era began in 1965. In the early years, large bonuses caused some concern, but the concern was short-lived. Iverson explains,

The first time we had a bonus that went over 100 percent, I thought we [had] created a monster. But that isn't true, and I am finding out that it isn't true because what we are doing is passing along to them [the employees] all of the labor savings that really come from the intense use of the capital in this business.

Correnti adds,

Do I care if they get more bonus? I think that's great. This is a capital-intensive industry. The more money we pay out every week or every month in wages, I am the happiest guy in the world. I am doing cartwheels. Because the more money we pay out in bonus, guess what? That's the month we have the highest profit because we put more sausage through that $500 million machine. The labor cost is nothing in this thing.

Everybody at Nucor is a businessman. They understand that the more money they make, the lower it drives our cost per ton and the more money the company makes. The lower it drives our cost per ton, the lower we can sell for; therefore, we can ensure job security. We have never had to shut down a plant or lay anybody off for lack of work. They know that by working hard and making money, they are increasing their job security. They are not working themselves out of a job.

Given the direct tie between performance and production bonuses, everyone wants to know where they stand on their weekly bonuses. At Nucor, employees do not need accountants to keep score. They keep score themselves. Mike Parrish says,

Our production people out there know every hour what their production is. They're predicting their bonus and posting it on their computer screens. They have programmed the calculation into the system. The base core production groups have instantaneous feedback on their bonus. They know how much money they predicted they would make each day, and they know how much they have actually made each hour.

During our plant tours at the Nucor Steel facility in Hickman, Arkansas, and the Nucor-Yamato Steel Company in Blytheville, Arkansas, we saw the predicted bonus for the day and the actual bonus earned up to the hour in the upper left-hand corner of the computer screens for each production group we visited. Correnti notes,

At the end of the day, the rolling mill clerk produces the numbers. They [the production teams] do not need a lot of formal information. They need a lot of hands-on, common sense experience. They need to know the tricks of the trade. Maintenance is critical. You screw up a piece of equipment, and you are in trouble. You are dealing with steel that is hot and heavy and sometimes liquid. If you mess up, you are not going to be down for five or six minutes, you are going to be down for six hours. Let me tell you, you just shot the bonus for the week big time.

Because maintenance is critical to Nucor's success, the maintenance employees are part of each production group, as are the supervisors, as mentioned above. If the machines go down, the production people, the maintenance people, and the supervisors all suffer together because they are all part of the same bonus system. They share the pain.

The Department Manager and Non-Production and Non-Department Manager Incentive Plans

The ROA-based incentive plans cover department managers and staff personnel at the divisions. It is the department heads and staff support personnel who focus on cost control. Iverson says,

> The next group is really the department managers, the six to eight people that report to the general manager. They work as a group, and their bonus is based on return on assets employed. When you slow a plant down from five days to four days, your ROA goes through the bottom. So the workers and foremen may get a 25 percent reduction in pay, but the department heads end up with a reduction in pay of 40 percent to 45 percent.

In the steel business, the only way you can avoid (or minimize the effects of) a slowdown is to be the low-cost producer. If the production workers focus on producing as many tons of steel as possible, then the department managers focus on producing those tons at the lowest possible cost. The lower the cost, the higher the division ROA at a given market price for steel.

The incentive bonuses for department managers and division staff personnel are paid annually based primarily on the ROA of their facility. The higher the ROA at each facility, the higher the annual bonus. Terry Lisenby, Corporate Controller, explains,

> The ROA people put most of their effort on controlling production costs and working capital. The biggest thing they can do is control production costs. They are constantly looking for ways to reduce costs. They post their costs and the costs at other locations for everyone to see. The competition between divisions is friendly because most of our more experienced people have worked at multiple locations.

Nucor's emphasis on cost control in the divisions is best illustrated by a story we were told on our visit to the Nucor-Yamato Steel facility and by their reasoning for keeping the headcount down to its lowest possible level. Both are related to the ROA-based incentive plan. Dan DiMicco said,

> Joe [Stratman, Subsidiary Controller] wants me to tell you a little story here about our ROA people, one of whom is sitting right outside the door over here, Kathy Jefferson.

> Kathy came up to me yesterday after picking these [two nuts and bolts] up off of the ground. A couple of our maintenance people were in the office area and had dropped them. She wanted to bring them in to me to make me aware of the fact that she didn't appreciate our operating people being wasteful with her bonus and profit sharing.

> I told that story to our managers, and I am going to tell that story to all of our supervisors at our monthly supervisors' meeting on the second Monday night of the month.

> That's the beauty of the system. You don't need five cost accountants to tell you to keep your costs down. You need 760 people being cost conscious, or being the human resource department, or being quality people, however you want to look at it.

Under Nucor's ROA-based incentive system that covers all nonproduction workers at each division, waste or inefficiency translates into a lower annual bonus and less profit sharing for all employees. When the ROA-based incentive system is combined with Nucor's no-layoff policy, the "beauty of the system" extends to headcount control. As DiMicco explains,

> One of the things you do to not put yourself in a layoff position is to not hire any more people than you need to do the job. Maybe hire a couple less, but don't hire more people than you need to do the job.

> If you are truly going to live up to a system that can support itself and reinforce itself in not laying people off, you can't let yourself get fat, dumb, and happy. So part of that philosophy is you don't hire any more people than you need to do the job. If you are going to err, err on hiring one less rather than one more. It is a long-term approach. That's a long-term philosophy. It enables you to keep true to your word about avoiding layoffs and not letting the system get out of control to the point where you can no longer take care of your people.

> If the management is fat, if you have more management than you need to have, what kind of example are you setting? You've got to set the right

example. Why do you think Ken [Iverson] is so particular about not going on junkets with suppliers, and not flying around in corporate jets, and not having private parking places, and not having separate cafeterias? He knows that you have to walk your talk.

Since information needed to run the production incentive plan is generated on a daily basis by the production employees themselves, the corporate controller and the division controllers focus on providing information on a monthly basis about where the divisions stand on making their annual ROA-based incentive compensation. Terry Lisenby says,

> We [at corporate headquarters] really operate as a service center with an oversight role. The divisions really look to us as a resource, more so than as watchdogs.

According to Joe Stratman,

> I would say that oversight and service is a very fair way to put it. Most of the conversations we have with corporate are about the business, more about general business issues than accounting issues.

The "oversight and service" description of corporate headquarters can be extended to the division operations as well. Associating the word "service" with "oversight" translates into a unique openness in management's philosophy about information sharing and communications.

The open communications philosophy is often credited to Dave Aycock, Nucor's immediate past president. John Correnti recalls,

> Aycock used to say, "You either tell them everything or tell them nothing."

> You either run a mushroom factory [keep them in the dark, cover them with manure] and tell them nothing, or tell them everything. If you try and do it halfway in between, then people worry about what you are not telling them. So we discuss issues in the open with every employee. Some people are afraid to let employees know how much the company makes and their division is making. We don't hide anything from them. The only thing we do not discuss with them is who is in line to be the next general manager. Those are all personnel issues.

Lisenby adds,

> We tell them everything. We do everything on a per-ton basis and do a consolidated report here, and we spread just the cost-per-ton numbers on every item. We distribute those reports to every division, and they pass

them around. They say, "Look, Texas is $12.50 a ton per alloys, and we are $14.00. What the hell is going on?"

Mike Parrish says,

> If an employee wants to come in and look at our spreadsheet or budget or whatever, I will show it to them. Here's where we are. There are no secrets. Everybody gets detailed and total information. Part of Stewart's [Stewart Roberts, Division Controller] job is to point out problems. It is easy for costs to get out of line. We ask questions. We are so lean that we cannot afford to have a lot of cost accountants on the payroll.

Given Nucor's ROA-based incentive compensation system, every employee is part cost accountant. Information sharing (both operating and financial information) and open communications are woven into the fabric of Nucor's day-to-day operating practices. The performance-measurement system and the ROA-based incentive compensation system are one and the same at Nucor.

The last incentive-compensation plan to be discussed is the senior officers' incentive plan. That plan covers the 5 officers at corporate headquarters and the 17 vice presidents and general managers in charge of the division operations.

Senior Officer Incentive Plan

Even though the operating vice presidents and general managers are responsible for the performance of their divisions, a significant part of their incentive compensation is based on Nucor's overall return on stockholders' equity. Terry Lisenby explains,

> We have the department manager group's incentive compensation based on ROA and the general managers' incentive compensation based on ROE. The department heads think efficiency. The general managers think growth.

As mentioned at the beginning of the Nucor story, management's overall strategy is to grow the business by taking market share away from the competition. In the Nucor system, "efficiency" translates into being the low-cost producer, and that responsibility falls on the shoulders of the department managers at each facility. The responsibility for growing the business falls on the shoulders of Nucor's senior officers.

Like any other growth company, Nucor retains most of its annual earnings. During the late 1980s and early 1990s, dividends represented about 15 percent of net income. In the past few years, dividends have represented less than 10 percent of net income. What does management do with the other 90 percent of earnings? It grows the business.

In addition to providing the money to grow the business, earnings provide a floor for determining incentive compensation for the senior officer group. The minimum earnings required for the ROE-based incentive compensation to be paid out have been raised almost every year since 1966. Lisenby says,

> Raising the [earnings] bogey is done here at corporate headquarters. Nothing is keeping that reasonable but integrity. Once we move the bogey up, we never move it down. Below 9 percent ROE, we get nothing. We set the cap at 24 percent.

Ken Iverson notes,

> If we hit a 24 percent ROE, the officers get 200 percent of base salary in cash and about another 100 percent in common stock. If you work hard, you have plenty of money to put away for retirement. With the part that is earned in stock, the payout is restricted to 20 percent a year.

> I remember that in 1981, my salary and bonus was about $460,000. In 1982, a terrible year, my total compensation was about $150,000. When I go through the plant, nobody asks why I make more than they do. They ask me when we are going to get production up to five days or six days.

Sam Siegel adds,

> In 1982, the officers earned $0 in bonus. Since we set the base pay at 75 percent of the base pay of similar organizations, the incentive becomes very important. When things are bad, everybody participates in reduced pay and profit sharing. If workers do not achieve their bonus (based on production per hour), everyone else will have corresponding reductions.

John Correnti notes,

> I get 75 percent of the base pay in the industry. When they [the rest of the Nucor employees] are doing poorly, I am doing poorly. When they are doing great, I am doing great.

> If we have a bad year, I am going to make $280,000. In a good year, I am going to make $1.6 million. You try going from $1.6 million to $280,000. That's the way the cookie crumbles, and that is the way it should crumble. Everyone should share the gain and share the pain.

In describing the impact of a business slowdown on the production employees and ROA-based employees, we mentioned that a 25 percent reduction in pay for production workers translates into a 40 percent to 50 percent reduction for department heads. What we failed to mention was the impact on the senior officers. As Iverson explains,

> When you slow a plant down from five days to four days, your ROA goes through the bottom. So the workers and foremen may get a 25 percent reduction, the department heads end up with a reduction of 40 percent to 45 percent, and the officers get a 60 percent to 70 percent reduction on their ROE-based bonus.

In an era when many companies are laying off employees while senior executives are making huge bonuses, the Nucor model provides an interesting alternative.

The Nucor Culture: Employee Relations

Without some idea about how senior managers think about employees, it would be very difficult to understand how these same managers think about business strategy, management control, and corporate account-ability. Like everything else at Nucor, management has a very efficient way of communicating its philosophy for interacting with employees. The incentive compensation plans are the most visible parts of the Nucor system. However, incentive compensation is not the whole story. It is just one of four employee-relations principles:

1. Management is obligated to manage Nucor in such a way that employees will have the opportunity to earn according to their productivity.

2. Employees should feel confident that if they do their jobs properly, they will have a job tomorrow.

3. Employees have the right to be treated fairly and must believe that they will be.

4. Employees must have an avenue of appeal when they believe they are being treated unfairly.[6]

The "avenue of appeal" that employees can travel when they be-lieve they have been treated unfairly is, in reality, one lane of an "open communications highway" that includes access to operating and financial information, as discussed. Open lines of communication begin at the very top at Nucor. John Correnti says,

> I answer my own telephone so that any employee can call me anytime, anywhere. It is important to keep lines of communication open and informal. The only downside is all the calls we get from brokers trying to sell us something.

Ken Iverson agrees:

> That is why John and I answer our own phones. We tell every employee that if they run into a serious problem, "You call us. Call John or call me."
>
> At a plant with a problem, they really call you and let you know about the problem.

Because of management's commitment to open communications, employees do not flood corporate headquarters with phone calls, but they do call when they feel they have been treated unfairly. However, respect for employees on a day-to-day basis and a no-layoff policy go a long way toward minimizing the need to call Iverson or Correnti.

Incentive compensation, along with a policy of no layoffs, fair treatment, and a grievance procedure, is known as Nucor's "share the pain, share the gain" management operating philosophy. Sam Siegel says, "We just do not think it is fair, other than for some differences in compensation, for people not to share in the pain and share in the gain."

Joe Stratman adds,

> It might take the total workforce population a little while to understand the system, but essentially they all do. It usually takes a plant to go through its first down cycle where the guys are cut back to three or four days for our system to sink in.
>
> Other companies are laying people off, and yes, my income is lower, but at least I have a job. Everybody still treats me the same way. I am not in fear of losing my job. I think it takes that first down cycle to really understand that. Here's why:
>
> Our system is no layoffs, but our system also says, "If there are down times, if the market is down, there is no production, we are going to cut back, but we are going to share the pain as we shared the gain." We are going to cut back somewhat equally. The production folks are going to get cut back to four days or three days of production or whatever. The ROA folks aren't going to get ROA. The ROE folks aren't going to get their ROE.

Dan DiMicco says,

> It's not that Nucor has not gone through tough times. It's not that we [haven't] been in positions where we could have laid people off. We certainly have been in those positions and could have, many, many times. But the philosophy, the system, the part of this that reinforces the whole system is that everybody shares the pain, everybody shares the gain.

> When times are tough, everybody is going to get hurt. Ken Iverson's salary can go from over $2 million a year down to $300,000 a year, and it has. Don't get me wrong. We are production oriented. We are cost driven. We are quality driven. We are safety driven. They all reinforce one another. So, the first thing to go is not the production. The first thing to go is the profit. The first people to be hurt by that are the Ken Iversons and Sam Siegels of this world and the Dan DiMiccos and Joe Stratmans of this world. The first people to feel the pain are the leadership. Not the other way around.

John Correnti describes Nucor's incentive compensation philosophy as "inverting the pyramid." The senior officers work for the department heads, the divisions, and the production groups. Under the Nucor system, the employees have to benefit before the officers receive their rewards. The Nucor culture is a bit unusual in this day and age, to say the least.

If we had not identified the individuals we quoted up to this point in the Nucor story, we suspect that readers would have had difficulty distinguishing the financial managers from the nonfinancial managers. Financial people are so integrated into the business at Nucor that they have the same concerns about the business as everyone else. To the extent that financial people bring a special perspective to the business, we can spend some time talking about Nucor's financial "organization." However, we put organization in quotes because Nucor is so lean that a clearly identifiable, separate financial organization just does not exist. Financial information and financial people are truly integrated into the fabric of the business at Nucor.

The Financial Organization

The responsibilities for the financial management of the company are shared between corporate headquarters [Sam Siegel, Vice Chairman and CFO, and Terry Lisenby, Corporate Controller] and the divisions. Joe Stratman says,

I think Sam Siegel and his financial leadership have been as much a part of the success of Nucor in the long run as all of the technological break-throughs. No doubt we have a visionary leader in Ken Iverson, who has had a technological vision of where the steel industry should go, and he has taken us there. But it has been Sam, more in the background, saying, "We will get there, but we will get there at the pace that will allow us to be profitable and be under control."

The pacing and control that Joe Stratman is talking about can be traced back to two primary financial management policies, one dealing with Nucor's debt-to-equity ratio and the other dealing with the division ROA targets. John Correnti explains,

What we do here running the corporation is make sure we have a strong balance sheet. The driver is that we are not going to let debt to total capital exceed 30 percent. The reason we do that is we are in a cyclical business. We run the company on a five-year plan, keeping in mind this 30 percent debt-to-total-capital ratio.

And when you look at our balance sheet, you can see that, because we are not highly leveraged, we don't have a debt service of $10 a ton or $20 or $30 a ton to pay. So when it comes time to get down and dirty in the gutter price wise, we can get down lower than anyone else.

As with any of its other costs, Nucor likes to think of interest expense on a cost-per-ton basis. The less interest Nucor has to pay, the more flexibility management has in lowering prices to increase market share and avoid financial trouble at the bottom of the business cycle.

The 30 percent debt-to-total-capital goal, along with a 25 percent ROA target for the operating divisions, governs how headquarters looks at the divisions from a financial point of view. John Correnti says,

Our goal is to earn a minimum 25 percent ROA [before federal income taxes and profit sharing]. Now we know we are not going to get that in the first or second year, but we had better be getting that by the third and the fourth years.

Lisenby adds,

I don't know where it [the 25 percent ROA target] came from. It was here when I got here. It's sort of like the 30 percent debt-to-total-capital ratio. We have done that for so long that it is almost ingrained into my psyche at this point. I can't tell you why that is a good number or even if that is a good number. It's just the number that works for us.

Ken Iverson notes,

> The 25 percent ROA and 30 percent debt-to-total-capital goals. Where did they come from? They just sort of evolved. For the ROA goal, we took everything out of the equation the divisions did not control. We keep it simple. You can ask a receptionist at a plant, and she will be able to tell you what the plant's ROA is.

Given Nucor's commitment to running a highly decentralized company, the corporate financial group (in reality, two people: Sam Siegel and Terry Lisenby) monitors the businesses in terms of these two major financial policies. The day-to-day operating responsibilities for living up to or within these guidelines fall on the division controllers.

The division controllers were typically referred to as being very "heavy" in responsibility. They are nearly all CPAs with public accounting experience prior to joining Nucor. As Lisenby explains,

> One of their biggest responsibilities is to provide information to the other managers at their level and the supervisors and employees below them. For us, it is not really important for them to be experts in accounting. However, our controllers are mostly CPAs. The importance of their training is to be able to understand a problem. Ex-CPAs are run through Internal Audit at corporate headquarters and then move right into controller positions. We typically get them after three to four years of public accounting experience.
>
> I think our division controllers are a little unique. A lot of our controllers end up being the "assistant" general managers. You have the vice president and general manager and the department managers (melting and casting, rolling, maintenance, sales, and the controller). Everything the general manager cannot do or does not have time to do falls on the controller because the other guys have specific operating and sales responsibilities. That's why you see a lot of vice presidents and general managers that were former controllers, because they really get a much broader exposure than the other department managers.
>
> If you hire people who need a structured environment, they are going to be unhappy campers at Nucor.

In addition to referring to the division controllers as assistant general managers, the term "division CFO" was used to illustrate that their responsibilities extended well beyond accounting and financial reporting. Stewart Roberts, Division Controller, says,

> "Controller" at Nucor is a misnomer. I spend between 10 to 15 percent of my time on accounting functions. I have an accountant who functions in

what most people would call the controller's role. She is in charge of all of the accounting functions.

I have responsibility for the personnel function, purchasing, MIS, maintenance, and, indirectly, safety, also credit and collections, liability issues, all legal issues. Most of my time is spent in the purchasing function, negotiations, legal issues, and personnel issues.

Joe Stratman adds,

This controller's job is an interesting position at Nucor. It is much broader than an accounting function. It is even much broader than a financial function. I have internal audit, both financial and operational, treasury, personnel (HR), data processing, purchasing, credit and collections, legal, regulatory interaction. So there are a lot of hats on the wall, and when you talk to other companies, you'll see that they have separate groups to handle these functions. We put a lot of the same functions under one person. We do not look at these functions as separate functions. That's just part of the job as controller.

In describing his relationship with Dan DiMicco, Joe Stratman talked about the type of person he would recommend that Dan hire when Joe moves on to another assignment in Nucor. Stratman says,

In looking at the possibility of finding a replacement for me if something happens, I said, "Dan, you need to hire an accountant. You need to hire a CPA. The person you hire has to have accounting so ingrained in him, be so used to it, so experienced in it, that he can do the accounting function in a relatively short amount of time."

It is more or less the no-brainer part of my job because the other challenges are so dynamic, so new to most accountants, that they consume more time just because they are doing and learning something new as opposed to doing what they already know.

During the interview with Dan DiMicco, the no-brainer part of the controller's job was reinforced as DiMicco described what he is looking for in all of his department managers:

Our first order interest is that we all wear one hat. We are all concerned with quality, cost, personnel issues. So's Joe. Now there are some basic functions that each department has to do. The shipping department has got to ship steel. The accounting department had better account, and the purchasing department had better purchase. In Nucor, those functions are base-level functions. They are important, and they have to be done right, and the manager's job is to make sure that they are done right. But the bigger part of their job is to work together as a team, to support one another because there are not that many of us. This is by design.

It is part of the system. And what does it do? It develops people to be more than they ever thought they could be. Joe Stratman is doing things today that, in his wildest dreams, he didn't think he would ever be doing.

Ever since we heard the term "no-brainer" used to describe accounting (and financial reporting) at Nucor, we have not been able to get that term out of our heads. "No-brainer" does not mean "not important" or "not valuable." At Nucor, everyone has a job to do and they are expected to do it right. Every job has a no-brainer aspect to it. What Nucor looks for is people who have skills to go beyond the no-brainer (automatic, taken-for-granted) aspects of their functional responsibilities and take on more general management decision-making responsibilities.

In drawing the Nucor story to a close, we would like to return to the words of Dan DiMicco:

It's the system, the system, the system. It's the people, the people, the people.

The key to our success is people and good communications. If you want to define success, you go back to some basic core beliefs and principles. The key to the Nucor system is that you treat people the way you would like to be treated. We are treating people the way we would want to be treated, whether it's our personnel issues, our interpersonal issues, family issues, pay issues, benefit issues, or how I work with you. Treat people the way we wanted to be treated. That's what the Nucor system is all about—respect for people.

Summing Up

If readers were looking for a story that focuses on the unique role that the financial organization or financial people play in Nucor, they have probably been disappointed. Of all of the firms included in this research study, Nucor has most fully integrated financial people into the day-to-day operations of the business. More open information sharing goes on at Nucor than at any other firm we have studied.

Although important, "measurement" is not a big deal at Nucor. What is a big deal is the emphasis on integrating people into the Nucor system. Nucor's management operating philosophy is grounded in its employees: All employees are linked to the organization through the incentive compensation system; the organization is focused on growing the business by increasing market share; and Nucor can grow the business by being the low-cost producer of steel and steel products.

The financial policies that Nucor follows were established by Sam Siegel and Ken Iverson shortly after they played "bet the company" back in 1965. Those policies (30 percent debt-to-total-capital ratio and a 25 percent ROA target) have been around for so long that everyone just takes them for granted. They don't question these financial policies because they work for Nucor.

The financial organization at corporate headquarters and in the divisions is populated primarily by ex-CPAs with several years' experience in public accounting. Their accounting skills represent the no-brainer part of their responsibilities. Their people skills are what got them to their current positions, and future promotions will be a function of how well the controllers, as members of their management teams, contribute to the overall success of their businesses.

After conducting the interviews and writing this case, we would not be unhappy if other companies started to adopt Nucor's overall management operating philosophy. The egalitarian approach has a lot to recommend it. John Correnti says,

> The Nucor system has evolved and been refined. The credit goes to Sam and Ken. I certainly wasn't like this when I came from U.S. Steel. But after 12 years, you look at the results. It works. It's a team effort. You also have to remember that most of the net worth of all of the 22 officers of the company is in Nucor stock. The last thing I want to do is shoot myself in the head or cut my own throat by changing a system that works.

Dan DiMicco adds,

> If Ken Iverson did this all at once, I would call him God. But what Ken Iverson did was bring people in to help reinforce a certain way of doing business, and they have developed all of these things over time. And now, when new guys like myself and Joe [Stratman] and others come in, we get the opportunity to reinforce the system and make it work better. How to be better leaders. How to keep it well oiled.

From our perspective, the Nucor story is all about being a business success, a financial success, and a people success.

People Interviewed

Ken Iverson
Chairman

Sam Siegel
Vice Chairman and CFO

John Correnti
President and CEO

Dan DiMicco
Vice President and General Manager, Nucor-Yamato Steel

Mike Parrish
Vice President and General Manager

Terry Lisenby
Corporate Controller

Joe Stratman
Subsidiary Controller

Stewart Roberts
Division Controller

Endnotes

1. *The Nucor Story*, p. 2. (This company brochure explains Nucor's management philosophy and operating style.)

2. See Richard Preston's *American Steel* (Prentice Hall Press, 1991) for a fascinating account of how Nucor got into the steelmaking business in the late 1960s and the early 1970s. Preston's account includes an interesting history of Nucor's evolution from its beginnings as the Reo Motor Car Company.

3. *The Nucor Story*, p. 4.

4. *The Nucor Story*, p. 10.

5. *The Nucor Story*, pp. 7–12.

6. *The Nucor Story*, p. 6.

4

BellSouth Corporation

Like each of the other case studies, the BellSouth story is part evolution and part revolution. The evolutionary part of the story provides a set of benchmarks that have helped us identify the "when and where" of the BellSouth story. The revolutionary part helped us identify the "why and how" of the changes taking place within the company. Revolutions take place when you change the laws, reorganize the company, and change the balance of power. Evolution occurs over time. It takes time to change a company's culture. It takes time to develop people with the skill sets needed to ensure the future success of the company.

In telling the BellSouth story, we will alternate between evolution and revolution. The BellSouth story will be told in terms of five critical events:

1. The integration of management from the BellSouth Enterprises holding company into BellSouth Corporation headquarters.

2. The creation of a CFO organization based on market-oriented financial analysis skills rather than regulatory accounting skills.

3. The deregulation of the telecommunications business, from "markets" organized by states and controlled by public service commissions to "markets" organized by customers and controlled through competitive pricing.

4. The shift from external rate-of-return regulation to internal rate-of-return (IRR) regulation.

5. The development of a budget-setting process driven by the market "expectations" of BellSouth's shareholders.

If we cast these same events within the context of the conceptual model introduced in Chapter 1, the BellSouth story may be visualized as shown in Figure 4.1.

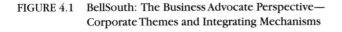

FIGURE 4.1   BellSouth: The Business Advocate Perspective—
                Corporate Themes and Integrating Mechanisms

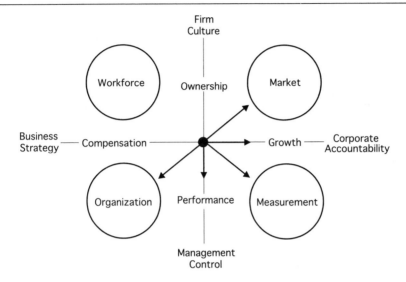

After divestiture from AT&T, BellSouth was reorganized to operate as a freestanding company. And within the past two years, the telecommunications side of the business has been reorganized into customer operating units (COUs) and shared resource units (SRUs). The financial measurements used to monitor performance in BellSouth Enterprises (BSE), the arm of BellSouth holding its unregulated businesses, are currently being implemented in BellSouth Telecommunications (BST). Throughout BellSouth, managers are being held accountable for the revenue they generate, the costs they incur, and the capital they employ. The changes occurring within BST are part of the management revolution being led by the senior executive team at BellSouth.

As a company, BellSouth has developed a market-driven planning process built around the company's three key strategies: (1) strengthen its leadership position as the premier communications company in the Southeast, (2) grow the domestic wireless business, and (3) grow the international business and expand into new markets. Although not mentioned specifically under the first strategy, the need to grow the business underlies all three strategies. BellSouth is also focusing on growing the value of the shareholders' investment. As we shall see, meeting market expectations for dividends and stock price appreciation translates into a need for "profitable" growth.

Markets, Measurement, and Organization

The way the market is linked to the organization at BellSouth is through the financial measurement system used to monitor the performance of all of BellSouth's businesses. The performance measures used on the unregulated side of the business are currently being implemented on the regulated side of the business. The measurement system that BellSouth uses to look at its internal businesses is the same one the company uses in the mergers and acquisitions process and assessing the capital market expectations for BellSouth's stock.

In BellSouth, the alignment of the organization, the market, and the measurement system is best exemplified through the budget-setting process. The annual earnings targets and capital budget allocations reflect a commitment to growth in both the customer and capital markets.

Let the Story Begin

The critical events that have occurred at BellSouth are all rooted in the break-up of AT&T in the early 1980s. If it were not for the break-up, BellSouth might not have decided to acquire and develop businesses that could operate in unregulated markets. If the break-up had not occurred, the BellSouth story would probably be quite a bit different from the one we are about to tell.

In listening to both operating and financial managers talk about the company, we found that one critical event would almost always surface. This critical event affected BSE and BST in quite different ways. Many managers at BSE were quite proud of the way this event has affected the entire company, while some managers from BST are still trying to implement the needed changes. The event we are talking about is the revolution at corporate headquarters caused by leveraging the accumulated market-based knowledge and experience of the management team from the unregulated (and substantially smaller) part of BellSouth with the knowledge and experience from the traditional, regulated telephone business.

Today, BellSouth is organized into two operating companies, BST and BSE. BST represents about $13 billion in revenue, BSE about $5 billion. However, even though BST is more than two-and-one-half times larger than BSE, the management operating philosophy developed on the unregulated side of the company is driving the entire corporation today. The new kids on the block in 1984–85 are now shaping the corporation! The old neighborhood isn't what it used to be.

A brief history of the creation of BSE and the combination of the BSE and corporate headquarters groups will set the stage for the remainder of the BellSouth story.

As Earle Mauldin, President and CEO, BSE, explains,

> BSE was formed in late 1985. Cellular [phones], the yellow pages, and international operations needed to have a place to grow up without being smothered by this $13 billion phone company [BST]. BSE then became the growth engine of BellSouth.

Ron Dykes, Executive Vice President and CFO, continues,

> Then in 1993, we merged the holding companies for the corporation and the unregulated companies. Earle [Mauldin] took over the corporate CFO job, and I became the corporate controller. One and one half years later, Earle became president of BSE and I became the corporate CFO.

Immediately prior to assuming their corporate responsibilities, Earle Mauldin was president of the cellular business and Ron Dykes was CFO of BSE. Mauldin says,

> After we combined the BSE and corporate headquarters into one group, the BSE holding company ceased to exist as a separate company. Bill McCoy [Vice Chairman], [Ron] Dykes, and myself then approached the business in a different manner. We installed a new regime at corporate for how we were going to run the business from a financial perspective.

> The fundamental business at BellSouth is changing. BSE is less regulated, but not unregulated. What has happened at BSE is affecting the entire culture at BellSouth.

The Influence of BellSouth Enterprises

The businesses falling under BSE did not really have to worry about changing an old, established culture. Most of these unregulated businesses were acquired through outright purchase or by forming joint ventures with domestic and global partners. Each business had its own unique culture.

Integrating corporate cultures was the name of the game in BSE because most of the new people joining BellSouth had never worked in a regulated environment. From the very beginning, these businesses with their "entrepreneurial" cultures were expected to be part of BellSouth's growth engine. They represented all that was new and different in BellSouth. Dykes says,

> I jumped right into the middle of the unregulated business side of the house in 1986–87. I got involved in developing our unregulated businesses. We were growing through acquisitions, and my job was to make sure the acquisitions made sense from a financial perspective.

Mark Droege, Vice President and Treasurer, adds,

> I came to BSE in 1986 and did financial analysis of all of the acquisitions for Ron [Dykes], using the DCF [discounted cash flow] discipline. Then I became CFO of one of our companies that was in trouble. I came back in 1991 as director of investor relations. Then I went out as president of a small cable business. It was corporate development–type work. Six months later, Ron asked me to come back and head up budget planning, long-range financial planning, and acquisition analysis [financial management]. On October 1 of this year [1996], I was elected treasurer of BellSouth Corporation. I kept financial management and picked up treasury and trust asset management.

Over a period of slightly more than one decade, the financial analysis skills associated with mergers and acquisitions were firmly entrenched at the top of the company. Now, the CFO and the Vice President and Treasurer are driving this market-oriented, financial analysis perspective throughout the entire financial organization.

By capturing the senior financial positions at the top of BellSouth, the Executive Vice President and CFO was in a position to build a financial organization that was tied closely to both the customer and capital markets.

Building the CFO Organization

As mentioned above, the seeds for growing a market-facing, financial organization were planted back in 1986–87 when Ron Dykes was building the merger and acquisition expertise that BellSouth needed to grow the unregulated side of the business. By the time we had the opportunity to conduct our research interviews at BellSouth, the corporate piece of the CFO organization was pretty much in place. Most of senior management's attention was focused on building the business-unit part of the CFO organization.

We begin this part of the BellSouth story by looking at the changes that have already taken place at the corporate level of the CFO organization. As we shall see, the people at the corporate level look at performance in terms of IRR, net present values (NPVs), and DCFs. Virtually everyone is oriented toward growing the business on behalf of the shareholders.

The Corporate Group

According to Ron Dykes, he did not have a grand vision of how he wanted this new financial organization to look. All he knew in the beginning was that he wanted the people in this new organization to play an active role in running the business. Dykes explains,

> I did not start out trying to put us where we are because I had some sort of experienced idea of where we ought to be. I just started putting the pieces together and thinking through logically what you need to run and grow the business, particularly on the unregulated side. So what kind of pressure do you want to put on things? What kind of relief values do you want to build into things?

The CFO's expectations for the kind of people he is looking for is reflected in the way he allocates his time. As Dykes notes,

> I spend less than one day a quarter on reporting and disclosure and most of that day is spent in interviews with the press on the earnings release. I do spend a good bit of time in front of analysts and investors, but that's generally related to discussing our strategies and listening to what they have to say.

> Eighty percent of my time is spent figuring out how to grow this business. I have one objective, and that is to find a quarter billion dollars of new earnings every year. We have got a business that generates $6.5 to $7 billion of cash flow a year. And all we have to do is figure out where to put that cash in order to generate that incremental $250 million of earnings every year. Now if that's your biggest challenge, why would you be focused on reporting to the SEC? I must have missed that day of class.

Like all the other firms in this study, BellSouth adheres to all of the accounting rules and regulations set by the Financial Accounting Standards Board (FASB) and the Securities and Exchange Commission (SEC). The question is not one of being in (or out of) compliance. The penalties for noncompliance keep everyone on the straight and narrow when it comes to external financial reporting.

The question is really one of mindset. Do the financial managers, who are key to BellSouth's future success, think in terms of complying with the rules and regulations or improving the business? In terms of our previous research findings, are financial managers Corporate Policemen or Business Advocates?

At BellSouth, the regulatory approach was pervasive throughout the telephone side of the company. BellSouth did not have all the people with the skill sets or mindsets that senior management perceived it needed to be a success in the competitive marketplace. According to Dykes,

> If you look back over the past 20 years, the finance hierarchy was populated by noncertified accountants. These were people who went to college, came to the telephone business, and the telephone business trained them on what they wanted them to do, which was a lot of regulatory accounting.
>
> At one time, we had maybe a handful of CPAs. And then the pendulum swung to needing to increase the professional quality of our accountants. This swing started to occur before we started to put the new [market-facing, financial analysis] paradigm in place. So we needed to hire CPAs and CMAs [Certified Management Accountants], and all of these kind of folks. Well, right direction, good intent, wrong target.
>
> Right now, we have to bring in people with seven to eight years of experience in financial analysis. In the future, we will be going for MBA finance and undergraduate finance majors in addition to accountants and accounting majors. We are looking for people who will be able to take a strategic role and drive this business forward.

At present, building a new CFO financial organization at BellSouth may be considered work in progress. On the unregulated side of the business, most of the CFOs working in the business units have the right mindset and work experience. At BSE, the development of the financial organization is virtually complete. On the BST side of the business, the business-unit presidents are still looking for the right "raw materials," people who can fit into the new paradigm.

In the discussion of the business-unit CFOs that follows, we have drawn primarily on the interviews with BSE CFOs.

The Business-Unit Group

The people who fill the CFO positions at BSE and BST will function more like business partners with their CEOs than like the controllers who grew up on the telephone side of the business. The change in orientation that BellSouth is looking for is currently being played out in the search for a new CFO at BST. As Jere Drummond, President and CEO of BST, explains,

> Our current controller, who comes from a regulatory accounting mode, does not like the confrontation with the business units and with [Ron] Dykes that goes along with the new CFO position.

> I need a CFO who is able to drive in and find the IRR, the NPV, the payback period. And then, he has to be able to differentiate the real opportunities and tell people that they did not make their hurdle rate and will not get their money.

> I am interviewing divisional people from companies like GE for the new CFO position. When you talk to those guys, you see the financial discipline in them, the participation in the business strategy that they learned from the time they started in the GE financial management program. Their career path in the finance division is amazing. I need a CFO that can be a strategy participant with me and support me at the senior management council level.

As part of the interview process, we had an opportunity to talk with Pat Casey, who was then Vice President and Comptroller at BST. Casey was quite candid about the role he played in the old regulatory environment and the role that the new CFO must play:

> I am going to retire from the company. We have seen the need for a new skill set, the need to develop a new partnership, and the need to develop a new control process. We have to be a more strongly focused and directive financial organization. The culture in the telephone company has been that the comptroller is a comptroller, team player, not an aggravator, not an instigator.

> The thing is, I am a born-and-bred telephone man. I am a controller, not a CFO. I am an accommodation, conciliation type of guy. We need a confrontation type of guy. The CFO has to be a business partner with a strong orientation toward financial discipline.

To a certain extent, the controller's role within BellSouth is dropping one level within the organization. Under the new paradigm, controllers report to CFOs throughout BellSouth. The accounting and financial reporting functions, although necessary, are not the primary focus as they were in a regulatory environment. Mark Feidler, President of Interconnection Services at BST, says,

> Let me tell you what I am looking for in a CFO. Number one, he needs to be able to drive throughout the entirety of my organization that we are going to make financially based decisions. That means I want to see the numbers on anything we do, from process redesign to the products we sell, to the compensation scheme. The CFO needs to be able to say that I need this information to measure the business.

Ron Dykes adds,

> Just to contrast with the old organization, we are in the process of hiring a new person to become the CFO at the telephone operations. At the corporate level, we have traditionally operated in this industry with a controller. His role in life was to look back, count the beans, see what we did, but rarely be involved in the business decisions.

> What we are trying to do is change that role to a much more forward-looking, analytical financial analyst. That person has to understand where the potholes are and where the benefits are of allocating resources in certain ways, be involved in the allocation of those resources to the various undertakings, and then have the status in the team to reflect on the performance of those undertakings. And if it stinks, he should say it stinks.

> We are looking for an accomplished CFO who is comfortable with this model. Given the nature of the changes required, we are going to have to rely on some journeyman experienced guy to come in and build it.

Rod Odom, President, BellSouth Business Systems, says,

> In my view, the CFO is not an accountant. If I got hit by a Mack truck today, I would expect the CFO to be the one most capable of stepping in and making decisions on my behalf to run the business. The CFO role is where the financial understanding and operational understanding really come together. The role and the purpose of the CFO is not simply to keep track of all of the numbers on the ledger. The CFO has to understand the operations of the business, where the business is headed, and how do we, through the use of a financially driven approach, really manage to generate the highest return for the business. My next CFO in my new assignment will have CFO experience on the unregulated side of the business.

As mentioned in the discussion of the differences between BSE and BST, BSE has been the growth engine for the company ever since it split off from AT&T at the end of 1983. And prior to becoming CFO of the entire company, Ron Dykes was CFO of BSE, the unregulated side of BellSouth. It was during this period that Dykes started to build the new paradigm for the entire company.

In the interviews we conducted with business-unit CFOs in BSE, the key characteristic that was common to all three CFOs was *operating experience*. They knew the language that the corporate group liked to speak because they were involved in negotiating the budgets for their business units. From their perspectives, they were where they were to do one thing, improve the business. And incidentally, all three CFOs were also CPAs. Steve Brake, CFO of BellSouth Personal Communications, explains,

> [At corporate,] I was responsible for organizing the due diligence investigations [for new acquisitions], gathering up the team (attorneys, engineers, marketing people, systems people), reporting back on whether the findings were consistent with the valuation that was put of the company, and all of that was communicated to officers of the company (what we did, why we did it, what we found, and how we dealt with it either through pricing or through changes in the negotiation process).
>
> In November 1995, I moved to BellSouth Personal Communications. We organized the company, built the network, created the distribution network, and went to market. We have literally built this business out of the air.
>
> As part of my current responsibilities, I have to manage the relationships between BellSouth Personal Communications and the 35 business partners we are working with in all of our different service areas.

Jim Glass, CFO of BellSouth Cellular, adds,

> I have a controller, a director of finance, a director of IFC relations, a chief strategist, and a chief information officer [CIO] reporting to me. I have strong dotted lines to the CFOs of our partnership properties. The controllers in each of our other businesses report to me.
>
> As of March 1, the CIO has to get out from under me. It's a huge operation. I can't afford to have my efforts defocused. I am concerned about our value equation. I have a declining growth in the revenue stream with more competitors coming in to further erode the price. The service is being commoditized and it is going to become more commoditized. Our capital

efficiency is under review and our capital expenditures are too heavy. Our cost of acquiring a new customer is relatively high.

At BellSouth Cellular, the economics of the business have been changing. Because of increased competition, the "value equation" Jim Glass talks about is not the same value equation that governed the cellular business in the past. To ensure that BellSouth Cellular makes money in the future, the CFO must reduce his span of control (which includes many functions other than finance, as noted above) in order to fulfill his primary responsibility. Glass says,

> My chief responsibility is to make money, collect cash, keep our costs down, and make sure that we don't lose any assets. We have to work very closely with sales and marketing. We have to be able to introduce new products for the customer, bill it, collect it, and service the customer. If we cannot do all of these things, we will either lose money, lose the customer, or both. We are here to make sure that things do not get out of control.

For a business-unit CFO like Glass, the key to success is making sure that the operations do not get out of control. His role as a business-unit CFO is different from Steve Brake's in terms of the specific management issues faced by the business units, but both roles require a strong emphasis on operations. As we shall see, Frank Lemond, CFO of BellSouth Advertising and Publications, participates in the business somewhat differently. Lemond explains,

> We own five companies. We have controllers in each of these companies that report to me. My direct reports have nonfinancial responsibility as well as financial. I have a controller (keeping the corporate books), financial planning and budgeting (including budget negotiations and business case development), distribution, collections, and customer services.
>
> I have financial and operational accountability. It's [my job is] deep and it's wide versus narrow and shallow. I ride with our sales people to see how the business is run. I am not the typical controller type. I have to make sure that I have the people who have those skills, but my focus is on operations, what we have to do to meet the growth, earnings, and cash flow targets set at the corporate level.

Before turning to the current management challenges and opportunities associated with further deregulation of the telephone business, let us summarize what we think we have learned about the CFO financial organization.

First, everyone must be able to speak the same language. Whether you are a financial person at the corporate level or at the business-unit level, you had better be able to speak the language of DCFs and IRRs. From that common ground, career paths within the corporate group are likely to be different from the career paths within the business units. And the only way to ensure that people do not get too set in their ways is to have them move between corporate and business-unit assignments.

If someone's career path consists of various corporate assignments, chances are that this person is an "analytic" type—good at analysis but with little experience in implementing a decision once it has been made. If someone's career path consists of various business-unit level assignments, chances are that this person is an "operational" type—good at implementing the decision once it has been made but not interested in being involved in the analysis leading up to the decision.

Based on the role requirements for a CFO in BellSouth, senior management is looking for someone who is comfortable with both analyzing and implementing.

Now we will look at why the revolution in the CFO financial organization has to get into high gear. The telephone business is no longer under rate-of-return regulation. The name of the game today is competition operating under price-cap regulation.

The first two critical events that we identified at BellSouth revolved around how the company was organized. As discussed above, the people from the unregulated segment of the company became more involved with corporate headquarters. Once in place, the financial mindset associated with growing the business through mergers and acquisitions provided the foundation for building a new CFO organization. Now, the CFO organization at the corporate level is pretty much in place. The CFO organization at the business-unit level is still work in progress.

The third critical event we identified during the interviews was the further deregulation of BellSouth's core telecommunications business. Although all the competitors in the telecommunications business had time to prepare for this revolution, the fateful event became a reality during 1996. Much of the skills and expertise needed to operate a regulated monopoly became an unwanted part of a legacy that had to be overcome.

As we shall see, the further deregulation of the markets where BellSouth had a virtual monopoly triggered yet another reorganization of the business. This reorganization, coupled with the influence of corporate headquarters by people with competitive market experience from

BSE, caused another shift in the balance of power. Where the company had largely been influenced by engineers and regulatory people, now the marketing and analytical (primarily financial) people were driving decisions. This shift in emphasis has had quite an impact on how BellSouth has been reorganized into COUs, how management performance is being measured, and how managers are being held accountable for the success of their individual businesses.

Customer Markets

In telling the BellSouth story, it is easy to fall in behind an organization that wants its people to be market focused and oriented toward the future. In our market economy, the future brings progress, growth, and prosperity. Anyone can look at the past with 20/20 hindsight. And wouldn't it be nice if we could declare a revolution in the way we are going to do business and wake up in the morning with all of the mundane changes being a thing of the past? Unfortunately, when revolution meets evolution, the revolution starts to proceed at a somewhat slower pace.

The unregulated side of BellSouth has had more than a decade to grow and prosper. The experience and capabilities of its leadership gave the rest of BellSouth the advantage of accelerating the needed changes. However, the changes have just begun on the telephone company side of the business. Rod Odom, President of BellSouth Systems, notes,

> Until three or four years ago, we had two distinct centers of power and influence in the telecommunications part of the business—the network organization (with power based on the fact that they controlled all of the money) and the state presidents (with regulatory and operating responsibilities).

Jere Drummond, President and CEO of BST, adds,

> Up to last year, all of our profit centers were states, and the states had authorized rates of return. We got all of that changed. We are no longer under rate-of-return regulation in those states. We are under price-cap regulation. So we are going to the profit centers being these COUs, and the other units are SRUs.

> Now we are saying that the COUs are the market leaders. It is a shift in the balance of power in the company. Historically, we have been network (technology, the best technology) and regulatory driven.

With the shift to the COUs as the market leaders, a whole new set of measurements is being used to assess the performance of the businesses. In the new organization, managers are held accountable for top-line (revenue) growth, expense control, and net income.

Much like those at Caterpillar, managers at BellSouth were formerly held accountable for not exceeding their budget once it was approved. As in any other bureaucratic organization, the trick was to get as many operating and capital budget dollars as you could and make sure you spent all of the money in the budget before year-end.

Before talking about how performance will be measured and rewarded in the future, it is important to understand just how different this planned culture is from the culture that existed until the recent past. Someone like Ron Dykes, who started working at the telephone company in the early 1970s and worked in the capital planning and deployment area, had firsthand knowledge of that paradigm.

For someone who is relatively new to the telephone business, the engineering and regulatory mindset stands in sharp contrast to that of a competitive market. Mark Feidler, President of Interconnection Services at BST, says,

> In BSE, we were very financially driven. The numbers reflect a lot of judgment. We come up with one business case. If it's NPV positive, it's a go; if it's NPV negative, it's over.

> At BST, on the other hand, where we enjoyed virtually 100 percent market share, there was little real need to have detailed, product-by-product numbers. Your main interest was total revenue and total expenses.

> At first blush, it sounds absurd, but as a regulated enterprise, what you wanted to do was to argue about the philosophy of things. When asked questions about cost, we said we did not know. We weren't lying to people. We just were not keeping the records that competitive companies kept.

> The last thing you needed to know is what a particular service cost. The regulators did not want the cost information either. As long as everybody is getting their phones answered and when a storm hits, it gets repaired, and it costs less than $20 a month, everything was okay.

In the new market environment, managers cannot survive without accurate financial information. The managers on the BST side of the business are now held accountable for achieving business results, not for living within an operating budget. Jere Drummond notes,

> Each of the four COUs we created will have revenue, expense, and contribution targets. We are going to drive it on contribution [i.e., excluding some allocated costs]. The businesses will be measured on contribution. The officers' short-term award will have a financial element that includes the corporate net income number, the BST net income number, and the net income for their area of responsibility.

Odom adds,

> I am held accountable for four primary things: revenue, overall expense, contribution, and headcount. I had the benefit of six years of having net income responsibility in BSE before getting into this job. On the telephone side of the business, we used to have third-level indicators serving as first-level performance measures.

Within the BellSouth management hierarchy, Rod Odom reports to Jere Drummond, who reports to the CEO of BellSouth.

The only way to put BellSouth's new performance measurement system in perspective is to compare it to the rate-of-return measurement system that most people in the telephone business have lived under since joining the company. The fourth critical event playing an important role at BellSouth is the shift away from operating under external rate-of-return regulation to building business cases based on exceeding internal hurdle rates (or IRRs).

The revolution has already occurred. The laws have been changed. BST has been reorganized, and managers know what they are being held accountable for. The only question that remains is how long it will take for a new measurement system to evolve. The longer it takes, the longer BellSouth will be competing with inadequate cost and profitability information.

Measurement

Rate-of-Return Regulation

Although terms like "capital" and "cost of capital" played a part in the rate-setting process, the key term was "revenue requirement." The interactions between BellSouth and the public service commissions in each state focused on approving BellSouth's "revenue requirement." Al Gasiorek, Director of Mergers and Acquisitions, says,

When I think about an income statement, it was exactly upside down [in a regulatory world]. We would tally up our costs; determine the amount of capital we needed, which we called our rate base; and then decided that we ought to earn 12 percent on that rate base. So profitability was a given.

But the process was one of putting the capital in the ground and somebody awarded you a rate of return. You would tally up your costs, and then magically you would calculate the "revenue requirement." So it was actually a backward sort of income statement.

Earle Mauldin adds,

Up until the telecommunications business was deregulated, our focus was on determining our "revenue requirement." You calculated how much you need, and you went to the regulators and made your case. Since we didn't have competitors, we were regulated to only be allowed to earn a fixed rate of return on our investment.

We would look at our current revenues, subtract our expenses, looked at our earnings, and calculated a rate of return on this growing investment base. Unless you raise revenue, the ROE will go down. So we factored in an ROE, worked it through the capital structure, came up with a needed earnings level, argued over the expenses, and then determined how much revenue was needed on top to get the ROE. That number is known as the "revenue requirement." You would then go to your customers, the members of the public service commission, and say, "We've got this revenue requirement." When they agreed or negotiated a different revenue requirement, we would put in new rates.

According to Mark Feidler,

The way you got the budget for the phone company was based on assets. You accepted the investment base, then debated the debt/equity mix, then the appropriate return on equity.

Now, we have formed a new social contract. We will not raise prices for five years. We will let competitors in the marketplace so there will be sufficient competition so that prices will be self-regulating. That's the deal we have called price-cap regulation. We are nine months into it, and as long as you get the cost out, you get to keep the money you make.

Using Al Gasiorek's concept of an upside-down income statement, a good part of the cultural change taking place at BellSouth involves getting people to think in terms of an income statement that is right side up. Under BellSouth's new financial paradigm, managers cannot start by specifying the capital they would like to have to do their job, adding a prespecified return, adding up all their expenses, and then determining the revenue they need to run the business. It worked that way in the past, but it does not work that way anymore.

Managers at BellSouth are being held accountable for the revenue they should be generating, the expenses they are incurring, and the net income they are earning in the short run. For the long run, they are being held accountable for meeting the financial targets specified in their approved business plan. And to get a business plan approved, all discounted future cash flows must have a positive NPV.

Internal Rate-of-Return Regulation

Under the new financial paradigm, managers and financial professionals must be able to speak the language of IRRs, NPVs, and DCFs. If managers cannot speak this language, they will have severe problems in dealing with the corporate financial group come budget time. From what we heard, people who have learned to speak the language the CFO speaks have fewer problems defending their business plans than do people who are having language problems. As Earle Mauldin explains,

> I had to learn how NPV works. NPV meant a lot when we got involved in buying a company and determining what we were going to bid. How much value is in the business. We brought a lot of that talent in from the outside.

> I am going to tell you how the tension works between the financial managers on the one hand and the business operations on the other. When we do a business case, there is a whole range of modeling tools that are used. The discount rate [which affects the NPV] has a lot to do with the success of the business case. Ron [Dykes] is the keeper of the discount rate, and [Mark] Droege enforces it.

Mauldin's learning experience refers to the time when he was appointed to the position of president of BellSouth's cellular business in the late 1980s. At that time, BellSouth had to buy a lot of the talent the company needed from the outside. Today, a lot of that same talent is hired away from the corporate mergers and acquisitions group at corporate headquarters. Al Gasiorek says,

> We have always been financially driven. We are just financially driven in another direction today.

> We [mergers and acquisitions] are being viewed as bringing good people into the organization. They know the language. They know how Ron [Dykes] thinks. They know the measurements he likes to see, the measures he uses to describe the business, and how he wants them portrayed quantitatively. People in the telephone company know that if they get one of my people now, it's an easy socialization job. Once they pass through here, they sort of have their ticket stamped. They know the vocabulary. They know the process, and Ron has gotten comfortable with them, having seen them work.

> I think that speaking the same language and using the same techniques and making the same assumptions is one of our strengths.

During the transition from an engineering and regulatory mindset to a marketing and financial mindset, BellSouth is finding it hard, but necessary, to emphasize a new financial paradigm. For some financial people who have been comfortable counting the beans and commenting on what BellSouth did last quarter or last year, the new language has proved to be a challenge. They do not fully understand what the managers in charge of the businesses need from their financial people. In those cases, the business-unit managers look to the CFO for help. Ron Dykes recalls,

> About two years ago, I took one of my best senior analysts from corporate headquarters and moved him to BST to start putting in place the same type of financial analysis we perform here. It is having a profound effect on the decision making within that group. I am not trying to teach DCF to the last man in the organization. I am trying to have some representation of those concepts at a decision-making level in the business units.

> I did not send them the DCF template. I sent them the guy who cut his teeth on the template and said, "You take this template down there, and you make it work." So we did a little missionary work.

The person Dykes sent to BST, Keith Tolbert, is now an assistant vice president for financial management within the network organization in BST. The language and analytical skills needed to operate under the new financial paradigm are being driven even further down in the telephone company.

Knowing what measurements the CFO needs to see and being able to speak the same language are important qualifications for anyone who aspires to be promoted within BellSouth. However, the emphasis in performance measurement at BellSouth is on *performance*, not measurement. If the business units cannot meet their business objectives,

Even though market expectations is a nice catch phrase to help us understand the shift from capital-based planning to market-based planning, we believe that the real key to BellSouth's new financial paradigm is captured by the phrase "so that the Street looks at us as a very stable producer."

Given the competitive nature of the unregulated side of the business and the new competition that BellSouth will face on the regulated side, the corporate financial organization has to balance current earnings with growing the business. As Ron Dykes explains,

> We do the budgets every year and review them with the senior management here [at corporate headquarters], and we compare them to the expectations of shareholders. Now the divisions come up with their bottom-up view. We have integrated the market-facing valuation approach with the budgeting process. The budget folks working for me are my buy-side analysts.

> My group will work independently, just looking externally, and about mid-year we will set out some preliminary targets for the corporation. The businesses at the same time are doing their bottom-up view.

> In September, I give the CEO and the management team my view of what the company should do next year. Then the businesses give their view. The official targets go out in October. In the beginning of November, the division presidents come in and give their views. When we get to the president's presentations, we set the final targets.

Given BellSouth's experience on the unregulated side of the business and the fact that the competition is beginning to enter the telephone side of the business, management is faced with a problem that most of us would like to have. BellSouth has more opportunities than it can afford to fund. The constraint on growth comes from being able to hit its earnings objectives. If all the investment opportunities were funded, earnings would be diluted and BellSouth could not meet the market expectations for earnings growth.

Ron Dykes and Mark Droege see their responsibility as balancing the earnings/growth tradeoff. When you are thinking about growth, earnings become a constraint, along with cash and people. BellSouth brings these three constraints together in approving new investments. Droege describes these as

> 1. A dilution constraint. We say that we just cannot tank earnings. As much as we talk about our internal perceptions of value, our stock is dividends

and earnings driven. If we miss earnings, our stock plummets. So we have a dilution effect.

After setting the earnings growth targets for the year, we can afford "x" cents of dilution and still meet market expectations. Start-ups really cause an earnings drain. A lot of small deals can really add up on the earnings side.

2. A cash constraint. How much money can we raise and spend without going below our minimum debt rating? So there is a cash constraint.

3. A people constraint. How many video deals or deals in China could you actually do in one year? We do not have enough people to do everything we want to do.

Summing Up

In our process of talking about budget setting, the other aspects of BellSouth's management operating philosophy that we have discussed seem to fit into a pretty cohesive pattern.

1. To understand what the market expects in terms of dividends and stock price appreciation, analysts need to know how to discount future cash flows and select the discount rates to calculate IRRs and NPVs.

2. The results of this analysis have to be translated into earnings targets and used to set capital expenditure limits.

3. Because there are more opportunities than there are resources (cash, people, earnings) to go around, some investment opportunities will be given higher priority than others.

4. If managers want to grow their businesses, they had better be able to communicate in the language preferred by the CFO—the person who happens to control the budget-setting process within BellSouth.

5. Speaking the same language and using the same analysis is one thing, being able to deliver the results is another. The people being hired into the business CFO positions must have a strong operations orientation. They will have to work with the other members of the management team to meet their business objectives.

The term that we use to sum up the BellSouth story is "financial discipline." BellSouth is creating a CFO organization that is responsive to the needs of the customer markets and the capital markets. The people in this financial organization are responsible for helping the operating managers achieve their business objectives and, along with the operating managers, are held accountable for achieving those results.

As many of the managers we interviewed were quick to point out, Ron Dykes has a habit of remembering what managers said they would do in terms of an approved business case. Dykes has a habit of tracking the financial performance of all investment projects that have been approved under his watch. He says,

> They [the corporate financial management group] look at all of the business operations on a regular basis. They provide me with feedback on performance issues, valuation issues.

> We have taken the market model and applied it to our internal businesses. They use the same approach as our mergers and acquisitions group. I do DCFs on every business every year on a recurring basis to compare their performance to the original business cases and compare their performance to their external peer groups.

> If we do not see value being created over the intermediate term, we tighten up the investment. So it is a pretty fact-based approach to investing in our businesses. It drives us to sell off assets that are underperforming.

On the basis of our previous research, we would consider the financial organization at BellSouth to be a true Business Advocate. At the corporate level, we see a little more command and control and a little less competitive team, but certainly no conformance orientation. Financial control is based on understanding and meeting the market's expectations for earnings growth. At the business-unit level (especially on the BSE side of the business), we see a little more competitive team and a little less command and control. The business-unit CFOs are there to help the operating managers meet their business objectives.

From a research perspective, BellSouth has provided us with an interesting view of how one firm is dealing with deregulation and increasing market competition. It has also shown how the CFO organization has participated in, or to use Earle Mauldin's words, "led the change in financial culture" at BellSouth.

People Interviewed

Corporate Headquarters

Ron Dykes
Executive Vice President and CFO

Mark Droege
Vice President and Treasurer

Keith Cowan
Vice President, Corporate Development

Al Gasiorek
Director of Mergers and Acquisitions

BellSouth Enterprises

Earle Mauldin
President and CEO

Steve Brake
CFO, BellSouth Personal Communications

Jim Glass
CFO, BellSouth Cellular

Frank Lemond
CFO, BellSouth Advertising and Publications

BellSouth Telecommunications

Jere Drummond
President and CEO

Mark Feidler
President, Interconnection Services

Rod Odom
President, BellSouth Business Systems

Pat Casey
Vice President and Comptroller

Gary Butler
Assistant Vice President,
Financial Planning and Analysis

Keith Tolbert
Assistant Vice President for Financial Management,
Network Organization

John Pappanastos
Senior Director, Financial Analysis

5

The Boeing Company

The Boeing story is one of a highly successful company in transition from being an engineering company to becoming a manufacturing company. This transition is born of competitive necessity as management positions Boeing to compete in a maturing industry in which profitability depends as much on cost leadership as it does on technology leadership. In the commercial aircraft business, the economics of owning and operating airplanes is not what it used to be. In the past, the company with the best technology for driving down fuel costs won the business. However, the ability to make marked improvements in fuel costs has decreased. At present, fuel costs represent only 18 percent of a plane's direct operating costs, down from 50 percent when the Boeing 707 was introduced 40 years ago. Thus, driving down a plane's cost to the customer means driving down the cost to manufacture the plane. This is Boeing's strategy for profitability.

The changes under way at Boeing are not born of crisis but rather of leadership. By no means is Boeing on the ropes. On the commercial side of its business, Boeing controls approximately 60 percent of market share. In the past year, it has made two strategic acquisitions on the aerospace and defense side of its business: Rockwell International's missile business and McDonnell Douglas.

The forces driving change at Boeing extend beyond those occurring in the competitive marketplace. Boeing has also changed its mission and operating philosophy. In 1995, under the direction of Frank Shrontz (former CEO), Boeing altered its basic mission statement to explicitly include shareholder value as a fundamental goal of the firm. Now, the only successful strategy is one that produces "profitability and growth as measured by shareholder value over the long term." Thus, a key challenge for Boeing management is to align strategy and shareholder expectations.

Another major change driver is operating philosophy, probably best captured in Phil Condit's vision of "people working together." It is not possible to describe or understand the initiatives Boeing is undertaking to improve the way it does business without reference to Condit's Vision of Boeing in 2016. Upon assuming his position as Chairman and CEO, Phil Condit laid out his Vision of Boeing in 2016, the year of its 100th anniversary. That vision goes beyond Boeing's strategic leadership to its operating philosophy. It is an integrated vision of the business, organization, and people of Boeing. It integrates the interests of customers, shareholders, and employees. This fact is expressed in the four principles that form the foundation of the vision: customer satisfaction, integrity, shareholder value, and people working together.

Many of the initiatives we will describe in the ensuing case follow directly from Condit's efforts to translate his vision into reality. For instance, to align employee and shareholder interests, Boeing established what it calls the ShareValue Trust Program, an innovative vehicle designed by Boeing's finance staff that gives each employee a financial stake in the company.

While the firm as a whole undergoes fundamental change, Boeing's CFO organization is undergoing its own transformation. Boeing's financial function has had a long-standing tradition as an independent review and budgetary oversight staff organization. This is changing. Condit's vision of people working together extends to the finance organization. For finance, it is hard to fall into line behind the CEO's vision of working together if the CFO organization is defined, or even perceived by line management, as a corporate cop.

Condit clearly expects finance to participate as a key member of the business team. Independence is still valued, but only if balanced by involvement in the business. While the CFO organization began this transformation about 10 years ago when Boyd Givan became CFO, the transformation has accelerated since Condit's appointment as President in 1995.

The CFO organization is involved in a series of initiatives to enable Condit's Vision of Boeing in 2016 to become reality. It has played a key role in the design of the ShareValue Trust Program. It is helping to build the systems that support Boeing's core competency in lean manufacturing. Financial people are being redeployed into Boeing's operating groups in small, process-focused organizations. Condit views Boeing's finance staff as a key resource for upgrading the financial literacy and business competencies of the firm's workforce.

Let the Story Begin

In telling the Boeing case, we will tell the story of the financial organization in the context of the story of firm-level change. The case will be told in terms of five key themes and the comprehensive set of initiatives Boeing has set in motion to realize Condit's Vision of Boeing in 2016. These five themes are

1. The maturation of the airplane industry and strategic initiatives to establish lean design and manufacturing as a core business competency.

2. The shift in mission to formally incorporate shareholder value and the ShareValue Trust Program as a key initiative to align Boeing people with that mission.

3. The shift to discounted cash flow (DCF) as the basis of the firm's value-aligned decision models and measurement systems.

4. The firm-wide initiative in business competency training and open-book management, which is intended to build workforce understanding of shareholder value concepts and the ability to manage using these concepts.

5. The restructuring of the firm's operating groups into small, process-focused organizations to achieve greater integration and accountability.

In terms of the conceptual model introduced in Chapter 1, the Boeing story may be visualized as shown in Figure 5.1.

The story of change at Boeing covers all bases of the model: the customer and capital markets, the workforce, the organization, and the measurement system. The integrating mechanism that Boeing managers stressed most in our interviews was stock ownership and, more specifically, the alignment of executive bonus systems with share value and the establishment of the ShareValue Trust Program for all other Boeing employees.

FIGURE 5.1   Boeing: The Business Advocate Perspective—
Corporate Themes and Integrating Mechanisms

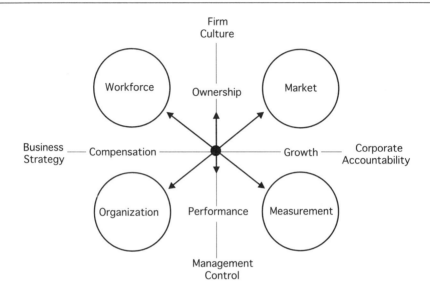

Customer Markets and Business Strategy

As much as the average traveler who flies in them may marvel at the technological wonder of the Boeing 747 or the new 777, in economic terms these products of high technology are considered to be commodities by senior management at Boeing. Boeing executives maintain that price and cost of ownership have increasingly become significant factors in competing for an airline's business. Phil Condit explains,

> As the product matures, the ability to differentiate your product from your competitor on performance characteristics goes down. For the 707, about 50 percent of direct operating costs was fuel, about 20 percent was cost of ownership. For the 777, fuel is 18 percent and cost of ownership is 60 percent. A 10 percent reduction in fuel burn only affects cost by 2 percent, and we are very near theoretical maximum.

Boyd Givan adds,

> We are a customer-driven operation now, and they are telling us that our products cost too much. So operating efficiency of our manufacturing processes is going to be much more important. We have an enormous initiative

under way to change the way we control the airplane configuration. We hope it will lead to significant cost reductions. But as already noted, fuel cost is no longer the major driver of plane economics. Couple that with the technological difficulty of achieving weight changes on the margin.

According to Tom Schick, Executive VP, Boeing Commercial Airplane Group (BCAG),

> The strategy is really being driven by a couple of things. I think it was recognized a few years ago by the leaders of this company that we were getting to a point in maturity in the airline industry and in aerospace industry that we would be becoming more and more of a commodity. A very technical commodity, but a commodity. In previous generations, the 747 was a leap into the technological end and so on, and you could look at different airplanes and see it. But today, we are pretty much in a very competitive environment, and the competition covers the total aspect of the product that we produce.... There are only about 460 customers, so if you are going to be very successful, repetitive business is important. Also, it's a product in an industry that is very influenced economically. We follow the economic turns dramatically as a cyclical industry and capital-intensive industry.

Tom Schick makes another important point with respect to Boeing's customers. They have become more financially driven, which in turn puts pressure on Boeing to become more financially driven:

> And if you look at our industry, the airlines are our customers. They are no longer being run by heads of operations or by pilots and engineers who really love the glory of the business. Northwest is run by guys out of Disney and Marriott. They're asset managers who look at airplanes like moving hotels to some degree. There is more of a financial view. I think the last cycle that the industry went through had a dramatic impact.... There is a whole different pull in the industry as to how you do business and what is important going forward. We just did a deal with Delta Air Lines, and before the deal was done, both the CEO and Chief Operating Officer came up— and do you know what they wanted to do? They wanted to walk through the factory to see what we were doing in the way of controlling and reducing cost and building quality, to be sure that the Boeing Company would be in existence for 20 years so that they could get their deal all the way through.

As the industry matures and customers become more sophisticated in their demands, Boeing is recalibrating its value proposition. It is not technology; it is not cost; it is not quality; it is not service; it is all of these. A customer value–oriented approach requires a balanced emphasis on quality, technology, cost, and schedule. No one imperative dominates. This balanced approach augurs a significant change in Boeing's culture and its workforce competencies. At the core of this change process is Boeing's world-class manufacturing initiative.

World-Class Manufacturing Capability

When we asked Phil Condit to identify the two most critical matters on his agenda of change, he was quick to single out two key elements of his Vision 2016: developing a truly world-class, efficient manufacturing system and fostering change in the mindsets and skill sets of the people at Boeing:

> The 2016 statement sets the post far enough out so people know we have to do some things to get there. First, we need a truly world-class, efficient manufacturing system. We have to learn how to be a manufacturer. The other for me is education. How do I take this very narrow disciplinary-oriented culture and begin that process?

As part of its strategy to provide better customer value and maintain strong demand for its product, Boeing is targeting on producing its planes in 1998 at the same cost it incurred in 1992—this means that at a 3.75 percent historical cost growth rate, Boeing will make its planes for 25 percent less in real terms in 1998 than in 1992. A significant part of that cost savings will be passed on to the customer.[1]

Boeing plans to maintain profitability in the face of real price deflation by significantly reducing the cost to design, develop, and manufacture airplanes. Cycle-time reduction achieved through streamlined workflow is the name of the game. Phil Condit makes no bones about it. He says, "We have to learn to be a manufacturer."

In his Vision of Boeing in 2016, Condit identified lean, efficient design and production systems as one of only three core competencies essential to the success of the firm (the others being detailed customer knowledge and focus and large-scale, complex system integration). Condit says,

> Lean, efficient design and production systems—notice I said design and production systems like *designandproduction* was one word. We must always think of them together. Our design and production systems will be among the best in the world with short time to market, short flow times, short cycle times, high quality, minimum tooling, and low inventory.

Boeing's world-class manufacturing initiative represents a complete reengineering of Boeing's value chain from aircraft design to acquisition of parts to airplane manufacture. The initiative has three elements:

1. *Design and Control the Airplane Configuration/Manufacturing Resource Management (DCAC/MRM).* DCAC/MRM is an integrated, paperless system for controlling the aircraft design and production. This initiative will result in a single stream of data and reduce some 400 separate systems and processes into four core systems. Taking into account that there are more than one million parts per airplane, this is no small undertaking.

2. *Make or buy initiative.* This initiative is designed to retain Boeing's core competencies while outsourcing remaining tasks. Considering that Boeing Commercial Airplane Group has more than 27,000 suppliers, this is a very large initiative.

3. *Lean manufacturing.* This involves changing and improving work areas for continuous flow and maximum efficiency through use of such techniques as kanban, pull production, employee involvement, and strong supplier partnerships.

Boeing's new value orientation extends beyond the customer. It extends to all of Boeing's key stakeholders, not the least of whom are Boeing's shareholders. The company has recently altered its mission statement to recognize its fundamental accountability for increasing shareholder value.

Capital Market Expectations and Shareholder Value

The shift in the company's mission has been designed to ensure that the emphasis on customer value is aligned with shareholder value. The shift to a mission explicitly linked to shareholder value is a story in itself. Suffice it to say that Boeing management came to realize that an explicit linkage to shareholder value provided an unqualified message about the company's responsibility to its investors.

It is not that Boeing has not been financially minded. Until recently, Boeing had defined its financial mission in terms of growth and earnings as measured by ROE—namely, to maintain a 20 percent average annual return on stockholder's equity. One problem with this formulation is that Boeing's stock price does not track very well to accounting-based measures of financial performance, such as ROE as measured by Boeing's program accounting system. And when senior management attempted to link its compensation to the ROE-based goal, executive compensation did not track very well with stock price performance either. This discrepancy caused many problems in communicating with the market as well as in helping those in management understand the relationship between their pay and shareholder value. In response, with leadership from the finance community in Boeing, the company changed its mission to establish a clear linkage to stock price and shareholder values. As Boyd Givan explains,

> We are moving toward managing for value as one of our fundamental goals. We had two fundamental goals: be numbers-oriented in terms of ROE and sales growth. It wasn't flowing down and did not make any sense. We have now changed that goal to increasing shareholder value over the long term. Everything we do in strategic decision making, compensation, and so on is now going to be related to shareholder value, meaning total shareholder return.

Boeing's finance staff has taken the lead in aligning the mission of increasing shareholder value over the long term with how the firm communicates externally with the capital marketplace and internally among its managers and employees. After formally changing its mission to emphasize shareholder value, Boeing hired its first senior executive for investor relations. Larry Bishop, who previously had served in this capacity at Lockheed, is now VP, Communications and Investor Relations, at Boeing. Bishop says,

> Under the prior management style, the relationships with shareholders and the professional investment community were pretty arm's length. The attitude was let's do what we have to and do no more. The function was assigned to the executive that runs our pension program. It was a part-time job.... Investor relations was part of a culture change that was already taking place. Frank Shrontz and Phil Condit accelerated the process. The culture change evolved out of the quality change.

Bishop's job has been to build a partnership with Boeing's shareholders by attracting the type of investor suited to its cycle of investment and profitability and by educating the investment community about Boeing's prospects and the most appropriate basis for valuing the firm. This second charge has been a major undertaking, since the earnings that come off Boeing's financial statements do not correlate well with the cash flows upon which its stock price is valued. This is because Boeing's financial reporting uses program accounting conventions. Program accounting is designed to smooth earnings from period to period by capitalizing aircraft tooling and preproduction expenditures and then expensing them as aircraft are sold.[2] Under this method, the unit cost is an average based on a conservative estimate of how many aircraft will be sold over a period of years. As Givan notes,

> Financial accounting and how we report on long-term programs is an unusual system. It tends to put things in big blocks for financial reporting, and for good reasons. It dampens the swings in the cycle, but it doesn't necessarily correlate with how the economics of the business work. In 1991 and '92 we had the biggest sales and earnings years in our history, but we operated behind the business cycle both on the up side and the down side, and the world was already going down, with airlines sliding deliveries and canceling orders. So we were laying people off at [a] time of record earnings. Nobody understood the accounting, which is also historical. ROE is working backwards.... ROE is out of sync with what is going on. We are trying to convince people not to worry about quarterly or annual earnings. It is, "What are we doing to increase the value of the firm long term?"

Boeing's financial executives believe that program accounting can provide confusing signals to the capital marketplace and to Boeing's workforce as well. As a result, they are deemphasizing the use of program accounting-based numbers when communicating externally and internally about the performance of the business. We will discuss the changes in internal financial communications that Boeing is making later. Regarding external communication, Boeing's emphasis on shareholder value growth over the long term and approach to partnering with its investors is being recognized by Wall Street:

> The company has complicated accounting designed to smooth earnings over the long investment and profit cycles associated with the manufacture and sales of large commercial jet transports. While program accounting may well be appropriate for very long-term aircraft investments, it also makes the forecasting of both EPS and cash flows much more difficult. The company is, however, much more investor-friendly and accessible than ever before....

> At the same time a new generation of Boeing senior executives is making fundamental changes in the way they view Boeing stock and its importance to the company. The company has begun to use stock price performance as an important measure of the company's overall performance.... The new, leaner, shareholder-friendly Boeing is not yet a reality, but the prom-

ise of such a company is so compelling that we believe investors must own Boeing stock.[3]

The Boeing Culture: People Working Together

According to Larry Bishop, Boeing's new approach to partnership with investors is part of a culture change that evolved out of Boeing's quality movement. The fullest expression of that culture of partnership is Phil Condit's Vision of Boeing in 2016. It is a vision of partnership involving customer, shareholder, and employee.

The heart of Condit's Vision of 2016 is the vision of Boeing as "people working together," which he identifies as one of four fundamental Boeing principles (the others being customer satisfaction, integrity, and shareholder value):

> Our strength will be in people, and our success will be dependent upon working together in an open, barrier-free environment. People will trust and respect each other. In simple terms, we will be able to rely on each other. People will value the diversity each person brings to the workplace. People will actively listen to each other, seeking to understand each other's point of view.

How do you marry the strategy of customer value and the mission of shareholder value with the vision of people working together? How do you ensure that the vision of "we're all in this together" is not mere rhetoric that clashes with the reality of creating wealth for someone else? This has been Condit's central concern. His Vision of Boeing in 2016 recognizes that a skilled and motivated workforce should be paid "at market rates with the opportunity to earn more based on company success."

After making the commitment to shareholder value growth over the long term, Boeing moved quickly to tie executive compensation directly to total shareholder return to replace the previous tie to ROE. As already noted, compensation based on ROE had proven unsatisfactory because it does not correlate well with stock price appreciation. As a result, in some years executives received lucrative bonuses while stock price was tanking and vice versa. The alignment between strategy and accountability was tenuous at best.

Boeing's financial organization had been the leader in advocating the shareholder value concept. The finance function had struggled to find the proper measurement system for tying senior management's compensation to shareholder value growth over the long term. Gary Beil, VP and Controller, explains,

> The task is to keep it simple. We were trying to get the focus away from financial measures to shareholder value growth over the long term. That was a real struggle. It took us a couple of years to get the acceptance and buy-in and commitment. It is now incorporated into the performance process. We spent a lot of time on this.

Having tied executive compensation to growth in shareholder value over the long term, the next step was logical: to provide all Boeing employees the opportunity to earn more, based on company success. Condit had been looking at different kinds of stock-based plans as a way to engage all Boeing employees and align their interests with shareholder value. According to Mike Stewart, VP, Human Resources,

> Over the past three or four years since Phil [Condit] moved up here as president, he has been doing a lot of work on employee equity ownership and looking at companies that do have some type of plan. And one of the things that he found and really one of our researchers found is that companies on the list of premier firms we compare ourselves to, who have some type of employee stock-ownership plan, have a higher degree of employee satisfaction than those that don't.

As Stewart points out, because of the cyclical nature of Boeing's business, its management has had a long-standing opposition to the idea of employee equity ownership. He notes,

> There has been in this company a reluctance to have employees tie up too much of their own personal wealth in Boeing stock, the reason being, if you look back on our history, we're a highly cyclical business. And so, Boyd Givan's predecessor, Hal Haynes, was really strident on this point. Our business and our stock price fluctuate so much that if your employees invest too much in your company, they may find that all that their [stock] value [has] eroded. Then what you've created is an employee morale problem. So there's a reluctance to have employees invested too heavily in Boeing stock.

The ShareValue Trust Program:
Linking the Workforce to the Capital Markets

Because of labor contract issues, among other reasons, Boeing had not been able to make the stock-option approach work. Under the leadership of Gary Beil, Boeing's corporate finance staff came up with an innovative alternative to stock options, the ShareValue Trust Program. Mike Stewart says,

> Establish a trust that is in the name of all of our employees with the distribution in company stock, and you're going to achieve that equity goal that you have in mind. It provides a strong employee-relation message. It became an issue of finance helping architect the best way to spend that money.

Paul Gifford, Director, Investor Relations, adds,

> Phil has always been an advocate of trying to make sure that in his vision everyone was compensated and had an opportunity to earn more on the success of the company. We had to find a way to do that. Right after the labor settlement, we seriously started doing stuff.

> The shift was made to the shareholder and to making people feel like owners. They had several alternatives within that envelope—such as stock options, straight stock payout, and shadow stock. Then Gary [Beil] conceived of this idea, which in reality is almost a perfect hedge. After your initial investment, your financial exposure ends. What you are forgoing is the cost of capital. Employees will look like owners; they will be owners.

To create the ShareValue program, Boeing established a $1 billion, 12-year, irrevocable stock investment trust. The investment is divided into two overlapping investment periods, each with an initial funding of $500 million. An individual's ShareValue distribution is a function of the growth in the investment as measured by total shareholder return, the number of program participants, and how many months they receive pay.

In its program announcement, the company provided some projected distributions based on varying levels of shareholder return assuming participation at current employment levels. At an average annual total shareholder return (TSR) of 15 percent, the value of the stock payout per participant in years two, four, and six was projected at approximately $1,300, $3,100, and $3,300.[4]

In announcing the ShareValue Trust Program to Boeing employees, Condit was very clear about its significance and its tie to his vision of people working together:

The ShareValue program. I'm excited about it. It's a major decision and a clear break with tradition for us.... I was often asked when I talked with many of you, "Why can't we share in the success of the company?"... We've been listening. And now we've tried to design a broad-based program where it's possible for everyone to share [at] a meaningful level in the company's success.

Together we have the ability to influence shareholder value. As an individual you may think you don't, but you do. It starts with taking time to become familiar with the ShareValue program. It's up to you. It's up to me. And it's up to all of us—to increase our company's value and then share in its success.[5]

Gary Scott, Vice President and General Manager, 737/757 Programs, is a very strong advocate of the ShareValue Trust Program. For Gary, it represents a major move "to change the culture and get our employees engaged." He continues,

We have had two of the biggest breakthroughs in the history of the Boeing company within the last few months. First, we finally came out with an employment stabilization policy. What we effectively said was that we will find work for willing employees who are displaced due to any of our new processes. And I carry that a little further and say you will get an equivalent or better job. We never said that before. Never. And you have to say that if you want to get the people engaged in supporting you and backing up your make/buy plans. It was absolutely essential. There was a tremendous push-back on DCAC/MRM, lean manufacturing, make/buy—all of these things—because they [employees] do not want their jobs to go out of existence. But they understand that sense of urgency to reduce cost/improve value. They are not yet convinced there is one because they still do not trust us (us being management). Without this policy, they just had a reason not to get engaged.

Second, the ShareValue program. We have always needed a way to reward people for getting engaged and trying to improve work and eliminate waste. We have talked over the years about profit sharing, gain sharing, and so forth, but to me, this ShareValue program is the best solution because it doesn't tie their rewards to anything that is controversial, like profits, which is an accounting number, or cash. And you do not have to get into a debate about how much of the profit or cash the workforce should get versus management, versus the shareholder. What shareholder value does is say,

"Hey, if we improve the value of the corporation, then everybody gains. You get a fraction of that because you have $1 billion now invested."

The changes made to executive compensation and the ShareValue program are concrete steps Boeing has taken to engage all employees in the firm's mission of increasing shareholder value. Many managers believe the ShareValue Trust Program is crucial to the entire change process. Beil notes,

> One of the big benefits to the ShareValue Trust is that it is acting as a catalyst for people to step up and say, "I have a right to care and a right to be heard, and there's waste, and something needs to be done about it." And so creating the pull for information upon which to make improvements in the business.

> So to the extent that the leaders are slow in pushing for change...there is the pull side where workers are saying, "Well, here's what I need. Here are our views." The ShareValue Trust Program is creating a lot of activity and interest from all corners. Really stirring the pot.

The Partnership Role of the Financial Organization

The ShareValue Trust Program illustrates the role that Boeing's financial organization is developing—that of enabler and advocate of business vision and strategy. Independence is still valued, but only if balanced with involvement in the business.

The role of the CFO organization is not solely a function of the CFO's vision. Ultimately, it is shaped by the broader operating philosophy of management. What does senior management expect? What opportunities does it provide for finance to contribute, and how does finance meet this expectation? As part of his vision of "people working together," Condit clearly expects finance to participate as a key member of the business team. His expectations are the same as those he had when he headed the 777 program. Condit explains,

> The design-build teams all had a finance participant on them. You were trying to get the designer, the builder, and the person who knows what it costs, and the customer and supplier into this teaming arrangement. The finance person was the one who put the numbers together and fed the information back to them.

Jerry King, Senior Vice President of the Boeing Defense and Space Group, shares his expectation:

I believe in the team concept, and, being an engineer, one of the gaps I had was on the business and financial side of the house. But the person I needed had to have an intuitive idea of the business. Our business has always been a cost-based business, so we needed to know our costs. We needed people who could be made part of the business team and had the ability to make business judgments and have them be held accountable with you for the success or failure of the decision you made. We did not need people who would sit back and point with pride or view with alarm.

Mike Stewart noted that these expectations of senior management reflect a broader shift in management operating philosophy that has affected all staff functions. In the past, senior management's command-and-control philosophy resulted in staff functions that operated more as policeman than as business partners. Stewart explains,

We had a different management control philosophy than we do in the company now. Much more centralized, functional control out of our corporate headquarters. That was not just finance, but human resources. It was exactly the same.... The same control structure and mechanisms that finance had in place, human resources had in place. And we were there as policemen on average labor grade, average rates, you know, hourly rates, job classifications. Our job was 75 percent making sure you held your thumb on rate escalation or grade escalation or anything else. As we tried to move away from that control mechanism, I [saw] finance doing exactly the same thing.

With this shift in expectations, the finance organization is starting to focus on help and support. Stewart continues,

That's the direction that I've seen the company moving. I listen to Phil as he has developed this philosophy. Then I look at the kinds of help that some of the finance people are giving us, whether it's merger-related issues or backing one of the operating groups. It's "We're going to spend the money, but what's the smartest way to spend it to create shareholder value?" Recently, the most visible form of this is the ShareValue Trust....

Gary Scott, a career finance person who made the shift to line management and is now Vice President and General Manager, 737/757 Programs, echoes Mike Stewart's point:

The way they are changing is that they (finance) are really becoming partners. All of the support organizations are becoming partners with the engineering and manufacturing folks in helping us met our QCDSM [quality-cost-delivery-safety-morale] goals. When I first started in finance, we used to just do what was required for finance purposes. Our customers (manufacturing, engineering, and the support folks) told us that we were of no value to them, and they were right. They needed to understand what things cost and what the cost drivers were and what changes in design and processes would mean. We started to evolve about 10 years ago, and today we have integrated product teams. The teams have finance people, manufacturing, engineering, support, all of the right elements together trying to figure out how to build a better airplane.

Scott's comments indicate that Boeing's finance organization has not traditionally stressed its role as business partner. In fact, Boeing's financial function has had a long-standing tradition as an independent review and budgetary oversight staff organization that no longer fits with the Boeing vision of people working together. Nevertheless, Ted Collins, Senior Vice President and General Counsel, cautions against too strong a swing away from the independence of finance toward the Business Advocate model:

You know that's changed a tremendous amount in the last few years, and actually it started under Hal Haynes's [previous CFO who held the position for 30 years] later years. It set a tone here. One of the strongest execs in the company came from finance, and he had some very strong views about the independence of the finance organization. And to my way of thinking, it's been one of the strengths of Boeing over the years, because the finance organization has been independent and able to say no when it's important to say no. Everyone's definitely into this working-together mode—we have to work together. The different functions have to support one another, but it is important to have somebody who is able to say no.

In view of these comments, it is no surprise that the mission statement of the Boeing Finance Function stresses a balanced role between conscience and consultant, fostering strong internal controls while providing reliable and effective support for the execution of business plans. But the partner role predominates. And the finance organization has made significant progress in making this role a reality. According to Tom Schick, Executive VP, BCAG,

We do not any longer, as far as I can see, make an organizational change without considering where the finance group fits into that so that we can see where we are going. It's a partnership in that operations still is going to be responsible for the operation, and the engineers still have to understand engineering. But they will do a better job because they understand the financial consequences of the decisions they are making.

Boeing's strategy of world-class manufacturing and its commitment to working together toward the objective of shareholder value are fundamental ingredients in Boeing's vision for change. In the terminology of Figure 5-1, the other ingredients—workforce, organization, and measurement—will enable Boeing people to create the success that they will share.

Skilled Workforce: Business Competencies

The source of Boeing's competitive advantage and the core of Condit's vision of people working together is a committed and competent workforce. The ShareValue Trust Program is a significant step by Boeing to build workforce commitment. Recall that Boeing's CEO, Phil Condit, identified workforce education as one of his most important priorities. As part of his notion that Boeing's workforce must become less discipline focused and more business focused, Condit has established a firmwide initiative to develop the business competencies of its managers, engineers, production workers, and sales force. Through this initiative, Condit is attempting to shape worker mindsets and skill sets.

A successful company aligns and optimizes its workforce skills around the core competencies needed to execute business strategy. Historically, an airplane's weight has been a major factor affecting its fuel consumption, and thus the economics of selling airplanes. Boeing's culture and management systems have been geared to encouraging engineers to reduce the weight of the aircraft. The emphasis was on the technical competency of building lighter aircraft. The economics followed naturally from focusing on technology.

This is no longer the case. The transformation required reflects the larger business need to move from being a technology company to being a manufacturing business. Engineers and managers need an enlarged set of competencies to meet this business need. Engineers can no longer afford the luxury of focusing on technology alone. They must focus more explicitly on the economics of the business, not simply the technology of their designs—especially since these designs affect manufacturing and, ultimately, the cost of ownership.

Thus Boeing's problem now is to alter its historically successful formula for building airplanes and to shift workforce mentality and capability toward optimizing a more inclusive set of variables that includes safety, weight, quality, cost, and service. According to Condit,

At the point of rapid change (propellers to jets), the thing that sells the product is the fundamental performance change (such as half as much fuel, twice as many people), and it tends to lead you to optimization around the things that the organization knows are those performance characteristics. In the Boeing Company, weight has always been a critical parameter for an airplane. You immediately have weight reduction teams. Everybody knows how to do it, and the competency to do that resides in a lot of people. Every design engineer knows what the weight of his or her part is.

The cost of ownership has a lot of leverage on this problem, but the people in the organization do not have the equipment to go work on that problem. If you ask engineers what this part costs, they do not have the foggiest idea what the part costs. They can tell you how much it weighs. "That's not fair, you changed the rules. That's what I know, and the organization is designed to work on those things." We can track our performance status just right on, the same for weight.

The implications are clear. If Boeing is to focus on cycle times and costs with as much fervor as on quality and technology, it must make sure that its workforce possesses the business competencies to manage this enlarged set of relationships, and it must empower its workforce to use this knowledge. One needed skill set is fluency in finance—the language of value, DCF, and cost flow. Condit says,

The engineer has to become fluent in finance. Fluent meaning, "I can speak the language." Not do it, but communicate in it. "What is cash flow? Why do I care what it is? What do you mean by discounted cash flow?" So that he knows, "I have got to go get a finance guy. I need somebody to come in here and help me look at this process." Is it better to do a machine part or not? We are going to have to add to the engineer's vocabulary, not just weight but cost and what are the elements of it....

In terms of developing fluency, we are going to have an education program of huge scale. In a company where functions were divided, if it had a dollar sign, that must be the finance department. We have some very literate engineers and some very illiterate engineers.... The education will be provided by the Center for Leadership and Learning.

This last comment by Condit alludes to the challenge Boeing faces. Financial illiteracy among engineers at Boeing stems from the highly functional character of Boeing's organization. Engineering has been the technical domain, finance has been the cost domain, and rarely, if ever, have the twain met! By reference to his own career development, Condit illustrates how deeply functional Boeing has been:

You are a product of your own experience. I have had a very wandering existence in the company, but it was totally nontechnical. I worked in Washington with the FAA [Federal Aviation Agency], then I was asked to move to marketing. I had my engineering boss's boss's boss, the director of engineering for the 747 program, call me into his office. He said, "You have to realize something—if you leave, you will never be allowed back. If you walk across that [functional] bridge, you ain't coming back ever." I did cross these boundaries. I wasn't smart enough to heed his advice.

It wasn't very long ago (about six years) that we had tuition reimbursement programs, and I had a big battle because a number of engineers wanted to get MBAs. The engineering department was turning them all down because it was not perceived by engineering management to be useful to their career development.

Clearly the challenge is not simply to develop skill sets. Mindsets have to change as well. Condit is looking to Boeing's Center for Leadership and Learning (BCLL) to spearhead this effort.

BCLL has a well-established competence in education and training. Boeing has provided world-class training and education to its customers for many years and has used state-of-the-art training technology including flight simulators, self-paced instruction, as well as classic lecture. In the following quote, Vice President Peter Morton, BCLL's director, indicates that the challenge is not simply that of building skill but raising awareness. Interestingly, Morton shared a different perspective about who was most in need of education. He argued that it was not so much engineers or production workers in need of financial literacy as much as senior management who must learn to trust.

People in a company like this have an emotional attachment to the product. There is an embedded intelligence in the employee base that knows almost instinctively what is the cost-effective way of doing something. I think the future of Boeing is finding a way of relinquishing controls in exchange for more information at the worker level and recognizing that there is no asset like a workforce that is informed, committed, accountable, and empowered. Somehow we have to find a way to deal with that.

The Contribution of Finance to the Business Competency Initiative

The ShareValue Trust Program was designed to engage and focus Boeing's people on the importance of shareholder value. The business competency initiative is designed to provide the Boeing workforce with the tools and skills needed to make decisions and take actions that actually deliver shareholder value. As Mike Stewart explains,

> Using ShareValue as the centerpiece, what we wanted to do was educate the employees on what it means to be an owner of the company. Consultants have shown us that the companies with successful stock-ownership plans focused their communication on three messages. One was that employees have a personal financial stake; second, they have an ability to influence the outcome; and third, they [receive] a lot of access to information.
>
> And so that's how we've been focusing the communication on ShareValue, and then using that to move to what it means to be an owner of a company, where you're the one making decisions and you're the one with a personal financial statement. And so that's how we've used that to get into Phil's desire to create this business competency.

The development of business competencies is a multifaceted challenge that Boeing has only started to tackle. Staff of BCLL are not tackling the problem on their own. Condit and BCLL are looking to the finance organization to take the lead in educating the Boeing workforce about the link between their actions and shareholder value. Boeing's finance staff has taken the lead in bringing senior managers on board. Tom Schick talked about the finance role in educating BCAG's leadership team:

> In almost every leadership meeting, Rick Swindler, VP, Finance, BCAG, takes a different part of either the P&L, or the balance sheet, or the cost structure and takes our executives through it. We call it business competency. So we have a business competency structure in the meetings that we have. We used to have a safety meeting, which we still do, and talk about quality. We have added to that an attempt to get an understanding at every level as to the financial consequences or aspects of how we do business. And it's important.
>
> You might think, "Well, why is that important?" Because in my mind most of the executives here were at one time in engineering, manufacturing, or sales. Their focus is on how we get this glass or this wing down the line, and how we do this and that. Being able to get a better picture of what that decision means for the company going forward is really important.

The finance organization is now working on an initiative to bring business competency training to the entire workforce. The financial organization's contribution to the business competency initiative is to educate the workforce about the goals of shareholder value, the concepts of DCF, and the business-case template that teams will employ in the decision-making process. Their strategy is a train-the-trainers approach. The corporate group is rolling out a company-wide training package on business competencies and shareholder value analysis. The initial target of this training is finance staff throughout Boeing. Once trained, these individuals will carry the training forward to the ultimate target, the nonfinancial workforce.

The intent is for engineers and production workers to start seeing themselves as business people. For this to happen, finance staff is taking on the role of educator—transferring their knowledge to the entire workforce. As Scott Carson, Senior VP, D&SG, explains,

> The difference that we made in defense and space, and is occurring in commercial, is what we call demystifying finance. When you talk about what we do in terms that the engineer can understand, all of a sudden it's not that complex, and they don't fear us, and they will ask us questions about "Now if I do this, what happens?" then you've won. You're part of the team. And they seek out your counsel, and you can make a difference.

This approach breaks down the disciplinary boundaries and barriers that pose possibly the greatest challenge to Condit in making his Vision of 2016 a reality. We turn next to these initiatives of organization and measurement that Boeing has undertaken to address these challenges.

Becoming a Process-Focused Manufacturing Organization: Of Teams and Tribes

Boeing's business strategy to develop lean, efficient *designandproduction* systems as a core competency demands integrated business processes. How will responsibility for managing on an integrated basis be established? Condit calls for small, responsive, process-focused organizational units. A key unit of action is the integrated product team. The model of the integrated product team emerged during the 777 product development program headed by Condit, as well as out of the program management structure used in the defense and space business. Condit recalls,

> We called the teams design-build teams. Today the name all the way through Boeing is integrated product teams. It is because design-build had this connotation that the designer and builder are there and everyone else is pe-

ripheral, as opposed to integrated product teams, where all of these people (including the supplier) are part of the process. At one point someone asked, "Why don't we call them design-build-support teams?" Then someone else said, "Why don't we call them design-build-support-finance teams?"

As the last quote suggests, finance plays a key role on these teams. This partnership role of 777 finance staff has become a model for the entire CFO organization. Boyd Givan explains,

> The teaming process really started with Phil Condit on the 777 project. You had engineers, and finance people who knew where the data was and how to get it to help the engineers analyze it.... The finance person's main job is to get the information, all of the data, for the team. As an engineer, Phil Condit knew the information system was not working well. Finance pulls all of the information together for engineering and manufacturing.

In spite of its obvious wisdom, the concept of the integrated product team runs counter to the Boeing culture of strong disciplines and functions. Disciplinary strength can be a great source of expertise and innovation, but it also has a darker side. Gary Scott refers to the dysfunctional aspect of disciplinary behavior in discussing the emphasis that he is placing on teaming:

> It gets back to this teaming issue—you need to find your reward in your work by helping build better airplanes. You do not find your reward by having this unique knowledge that people have to come knocking on your door to get. Which has sort of the way it has been.

Condit is quite emphatic about the need to break down the functional walls that exist at Boeing, but he also is realistic about how far he can take this:

> I think that we have to start from the premise that human beings are tribal in their genetic code. I think it is communication driven. There are only a certain number of people that we can know well and therefore trust and that becomes "us." If you watch an organization, it will divide up into tribes, and some of them are real easy to figure out. We tend to congregate with people that are like us. So finance forms their tribe, and engineers form their tribe.... I have watched people go from Everett to Renton or Renton to Everett—our two big, identical, mirror-image, assembly divisions—and they can switch literally in a matter of days to who's "us" and who's "them."
>
> I start with the premise the tribal instinct is natural behavior. Left to its devices, it will go that way. So you then have to build mechanisms to promote and then sustain trust. We used a lot of working-together teams,

and they try to go across functions. One of the interesting things that has happened already is that some people say, "I see how this thing works. We are not going to be finance and engineering and planning and tooling any more. We are going to be teams." So the tribe is being redefined. Every team has a functional member. We just changed the walls. We had the walls going this way, now we have the walls going this other way.

The Matrix Organization

As Boeing moves toward highly integrated, efficient business processes performed by cross-functional teams, it is also decentralizing its operations through use of the matrix model. While many firms have tried and failed to make the matrix model work, Boeing is hoping to draw on its successful use of the matrix model in the defense and space business. Gary Scott notes,

> Today, we are very matrixed. We have actually moved to look more like defense and space. In the old days, we had a separate 737/757 company that acted totally different than the large 747/767 company. It was really good from a command-and-control standpoint. You had total control. It was easy. I could just tell you what to do. Now we really all have to work together. The common commitment is to building a good plane. The fundamental problem with the command-and-control system was that it was very expensive. We had redundancies everywhere. It was comfortable, but we cannot afford it today. The matrix organization is much more efficient, but it requires a new mindset of working together.

Curt Nohavec, Assistant Controller for Operations Planning, explains how the matrix will work, including the involvement of finance staff, and how it differs from the way the commercial side of business has been organized:

> The wing responsibility center will have responsibility for designing and building wings. They will have performance commitments and performance management plans. They will have finance representation through a finance manager. In the old days, there was no breakdown below the plane level. Today, the 777 program team will be responsible for contracting with the wing group for the wings they need. The 747 team will also contract with the wing people. Now the wing group has a 25 percent cost reduction target along with other responsibility centers....

The matrix approach represents a dramatic change in the way the firm is organized. It demands an equally dramatic change in Boeing's measurement systems. Nohavec continues,

The old finance systems were designed as an "up-and-out" vertical process. You could tell how much money a functional unit spent, but you could not tell how much it cost to build this wing. DCAC/MRM will give us a much better understanding of what process costs are all about. When you get down to these business units, this will give them the information they need to balance weight, cost, and cycle time.

Why the switch? The idea is that smaller, more accountable organizations make for more productive units of action. The challenge is to make sure these small units act in an integrated fashion around the needs of the product and customer. Otherwise the firm will disintegrate. Boeing executives emphasize the importance of mindset and culture as key integrative forces to ensure that Boeing's smaller, matrixed units are guided in their local actions by a global, product-oriented perspective. As Tom Schick explains,

We started with integrated product teams and business units. What we are doing is making more bite-size, controllable pieces out on the factory floor. That is important because it kind of gives them ownership and empowerment as to how to handle it, but historically they haven't always known what it costs to do things. Our finance department today is more and more making that visibility available and allowing decisions to be made on business or financial or economic terms.

Gary Scott adds,

I am convinced that you can't get an organization more than a certain size to perform. The whole concept of lean manufacturing is based on small business units. It gets right back to having the right culture. You have to want to work together, and you have to have the right mindset. You can't ever forget, however, that you have to look at everything from the program end of the microscope. And if you ever forget that and if you ever think that you are just in the wing business, and you forget that it has to be integrated with the other parts of the plane, you are in trouble.

The Process Focus of the Finance Organization

The move to create smaller, process-focused organizational units affects the finance organization in two significant ways. First, in keeping with the broader firm initiative, the finance organization is becoming more process focused. As part of this process orientation, finance staff are increasingly expected to provide integrated services to the business team. Second, as the firm drives decision making and accountability down into the organization, the demand for finance staff and financial information increases exponentially.

The financial organization is currently wrestling with how best to respond to this demand. It is trying to find the right balance between centralized systems and services and decentralized staff who participate on the business-unit teams. Rick Swindler, Vice President of Finance for BCAG, is responsible for striking this balance. He explains,

> We said that our strategy is to continue to develop a process-driven finance business management organization.... The processes I'm talking about are the "finance" processes.... How we do budgeting, how we pay our bills, the business planning process, the financial planning process, and so on.

> We have a strategy in the Boeing Company that says we're going to go with small, responsive, process-focused organizations. And we have a strategy that says in some cases we're going to have small, central organizations.... For example, let's say we're going to focus on the processes to build the wing, the wing responsibility center. But meanwhile, the rest of the processes that support the wing plus a bunch of other processes ought to all be done the same. Most of our finance processes are like that. So even though we'll have people out with the wing, we need to have common, efficient processes.

As BCAG's finance organization restructures itself to better serve the group's new matrix structure, it is defining new roles and struggling to manage a potentially higher cost structure. The enriched staffing requirement for this initiative is troublesome, especially in light of Boeing's strong push to control costs. Swindler continues,

> We're breaking the enterprise into business units. One of our initiatives in finance is how to best support the business-unit structure and do the "Business Advocate" role better. And there's a new title that we're using around here called business analyst; we are spending a lot of time defining what the role of the business analyst should be. It is putting these business analysts in the business units and saying it is their job to help place a focus on the cost drivers of the business unit—to use tools like activity-based costing to help them in their process management activities as part of continuous quality improvement.

> We're also having to build our staff somewhat, which some people aren't totally comfortable with. I have stated from the very beginning that this business-unit approach is a wonderful strategy, but expensive for support functions. A.T. Kearny did some benchmarking of finance and showed that finance costs as a percent of revenue are much higher in decentralized

firms. So I said, when you use a decentralized approach, it's going to cost you something, and particularly if we're going to really do more than we've been doing before as far as helping identify cost drivers. It's going to mean more people in finance. Overall, of course, the intent is less total cost.

The plan and the hope are that, as Boeing succeeds in its various systems initiatives that deliver integrated information directly to engineering and production teams, the demand for financial staff will ease. This is clearly the strategy on the defense and aerospace side of Boeing.

The defense and commercial sides of Boeing differ in that the defense business has pursued a strategy of decentralization for some years now. So as D&SG implements integrated systems, it is positioned to take advantage of the staffing efficiencies that might result. The commercial business is just making the commitment to decentralization and so must ramp up its finance staffing requirements in the short term before seeing any long-term efficiencies from its systems improvements.

Business Integration

As Boeing evolves to a more integrated way of managing based on business processes, there appears to be a natural evolution toward integrating the various staff functions. The role evolving at Boeing is that of the business resources manager. In essence, at the business-unit level, the business resources manager functions as a chief financial and administrative officer. The role evolved first in D&SG and has recently been adopted by BCAG. Scott Carson, appointed in 1996 to be Senior Vice President, Business Management, for D&SG, is a long-time advocate and architect of the business resources concept. He says,

> Our world was really funny. So much of what we did was what I would call cost management, cost reporting, and we confused ourselves, thinking we did that largely for our customer. And it wasn't until sometime in the 1980s that we decided this whole cost management job that we did was part of program management and started changing the way we thought about the problem.

> Like a lot of companies that came out of the postwar era, we had gone through this very chimneyed specialization, which drives exactly what we are talking about. As we started to see, the need was for people to integrate cost data with scheduled data, with contractual information.... All of our significant management people are folks that are multilingual in terms of their capability.

Carson and his colleagues experimented with the concept as part of the management team of the Space Station project. The whole idea was to produce better information for better management decisions. Bob Ingersoll, who is currently in charge of all business management issues in connection with the merger of Boeing and McDonnell Douglas, describes the innovations they put in place. The business resources manager represents the essence of the Business Advocate—service, involvement, and business integration. Ingersoll says,

> One of the enjoyable parts of my job when I was on Space Station being the business manager was to lead what we call an integrated business team. And that, I think, is kind of a front-runner of where the business community is headed in finance and the business.... It's the process-driven team approach. Our mission was to develop the business plan for the Space Station—whether it be the accounting, the estimating, the contracting, scheduling. It was all there. We were all colocated. We basically took our titles off. I mean, you sat down at a meeting, and you really didn't know which one was the finance person, or the procurement person, or the scheduler. Because we were all working on common issues, but we brought in expertise from our backgrounds, and to me, looking at the synergy of that and the outcome of it, it was very positive.

The job of the business resources manager represented a major shift of orientation from function to process and from oversight to service. Ingersoll continues,

> Before, a function had a charter. They went and did their thing. Now they have a customer—an internal customer—and that's the program manager, and you look at that person as a customer. I'm here to provide you a service. I want you to be satisfied, happy with what I'm doing as opposed to what it used to be: "I'm going to keep you out of jail whether you like it or not."

Carson tried to sell the idea to senior management at D&SG, but the timing was not right. He explains,

> We actually spent a lot of time in the late 1980s thinking about the need for this integrated function. We have written a small book that describes how these organizations would work. I gave that book to Jack Byeman and Fred Howard (BCAG) in 1991 when I couldn't sell it here at D&SG. The integrated function included planning, as in scheduling, industrial engineering, and those kinds of things. Because we had gotten so fractured, we did cost management in finance, we did cost management in material, we did cost management in manufacturing and in engineering, and never integrated even the cost-management activity. And then we did scheduling as a sepa-

rate organization across those same units. As we were cutting back, we went from 60,000 people to 29,000 people in five years. One of the fears was, can we make those cuts and not lose control? And the only way we could see to do that was to start marrying organizations.

Good ideas stand the test of time. BCAG management picked up on Carson's ideas, and with the recent change in management at D&SG, the business resources management concept represents the new paradigm for the organization of administrative support services. Mike Stewart, who was head of Employee Relations for BCAG, discusses the adoption of the business resources manager concept:

> We did something else in commercial that was beneficial at the senior management level. I don't know how much it contributed to the lower end of the organization, but we put together what was called the Business Resources Organization under Fred Howard. And within Business Resources, as one of the macro processes in commercial, we had finance, human resources, computing, facilities, program management, and a couple of other minor things. But essentially it was taking a whole systems look at all the resources that are provided to run the business. Whether it was people or facilities or computing, all of those things [came] under the umbrella of Business Resources. And so we would find ourselves making decisions together. Computing and facilities and people with the help of a finance person, kind of looking across the entire spectrum of resource requirements.

Tom Schick also commented on the new position of VP for Business Resources:

> He has finance, he has contracts, and so on.... The way I look at it, what Fred has in this organization are all of the things that impact and aid in decisions going forward by the line guys. And they, all of them, to some degree or another are financially oriented.

Scott Carson emphasizes the newness of the changes he has made upon his recent appointment to a comparable position for D&SG. Finance as business integrator is the defining concept. He says,

> This structure is really new. We have five sectors in the new organization. In each of those five sectors, I have a senior business resources person. In three of the five sectors, those are people that were senior finance people but have had broad experience. One of them is a contracts person that has the same broad experience, and one we are still competing. But, in each of those sectors, we have a position that looks a lot like mine. They may have different things that report to them, but the notion that they integrate the

business information on behalf of the general manager of that sector is what's key.

Boeing's concept of the business resources manager is still evolving. For instance, it is not clear how the adoption of the business resources manager at the group and division level will play out at lower organizational levels. As mentioned earlier, Rick Swindler, who reports to Fred Howard, is helping to define the business analyst role of the finance person who supports the decentralized product teams and management business units. He is not certain that the generalist orientation of the business resources manager advocated by Scott Carson is an appropriate or feasible model for the business analyst. Swindler says,

> That's what Scott does now. And that's what Fred Howard does. I think it would be a good idea to have some generalists that could then help in the delivery of all the business stuff like Scott is talking about, but I think it will be complicated enough for business analysts to know enough about all of finance—to know where to get all the help just with our finance processes to begin with, much less contracts and information systems and all the rest of it.

Because the business analyst operates at a much lower level of the organization, Swindler sees this role as more specialized and finance focused than the business resources management role, with its responsibility to integrate all support services. The people who fill the role of business analyst are focused on helping product teams and front-line workers understand their cost drivers as well as the financial consequences of their actions. While they are addressing support staffing needs at different levels of the organization, clearly Swindler and Carson share an emphasis on business integration.

Performance Measurement

In view of the foregoing initiatives, Boeing faces two major measurement system challenges: aligning its decision models and performance measurement systems with the objective of shareholder value and aligning its information systems with the new structure of decentralized organizational accountability.

The major preoccupation of finance staff has been with ensuring that the discipline of shareholder value becomes firmly established in

Boeing's decision-making process. As previously described, Boeing's business competency initiative is to educate the workforce about the goals of shareholder value, the concepts of DCF, and the business-case template that teams will employ in the decision-making process. At this juncture, the shareholder value framework is fairly well embedded in the capital budgeting and operating plan processes at the division level. Swindler describes how shareholder value concepts have been embedded in the annual business planning process:

> When we do our business plan—and the Defense and Space Group is the same way—we have to identify our major strategies leading up to a major presentation from us to Phil…. We identify our major strategies, we identify our major initiatives, we do a financial forecast, including future cash flows, and then we discount that back and say here's the value of BCAG, total BCAG. And then we say, "Okay now, what's the impact of these major strategies on that value?"

> And when we wrap up year-end performance, we review that with Phil and we say, "Here's where we started with shareholder value, here's where we ended, on a corporate-wide basis, and here's the financial view of why some of those things happened, here's what management did to influence the increase, here's what happened in the external environment." Growth in shareholder value is built into two places. It's built into our BCAG performance commitment to Phil, and it comprises 30 percent of the executive bonus, based on the total Boeing evaluation. So, shareholder value has definitely been integrated into performance management around here.

The next step in integrating shareholder value into the performance measurement system is to make sure it flows down below the group level. For instance, at this point Boeing does not track product program investments that are justified using shareholder value analysis. This is changing in D&SG, which has an initiative to do so. As Carson explains,

> We have never tracked capital projects, and even on some of these new commercial miniatures that we have started, the attitude tends to be, well, when we committed to it we were going to make 30 percent, but now those costs are sunk…. And yet, if you go back and review the whole business case, you find that the measure really doesn't look very attractive. I want to know that when I make the next decision…because if you make a whole series of bad decisions by discounting and throwing away this sunk cost, it hurts the enterprise.

> And I am big on accountability, not in an adversarial way but in a partnership way, so that you're making decisions…. We are working really hard on

a tool; it will be the first tool that we have had that will really allow us to do project-by-project cash flow. And not only to justify the project, which you've done in the past, but to track it.

Visibility, Ownership, and Openness

As Boeing moves toward making its workers full partners by providing them a financial stake in the business, by empowering them to manage their own work, and by holding them accountable for results, it is also making information available in a much more open way than it ever has before. Open-book management represents the intersection of culture and measurement. It is one topic that Boeing executives talk about frequently because it is not in their heritage: Boeing's heritage is one of tight control over information. In view of this culture of tight control, Boeing managers understand that there is a natural resistance to openness that they must confront directly.

Gary Beil draws the connections between the ShareValue Trust Program, the business competency initiatives, and open-book management. Beil talks about Boeing's efforts to educate its workforce about the business as part of the ShareValue Trust Program:

> We're going to be challenged by the open-book concept. It started out as a communication initiative for the ShareValue Trust Program. But it's a lot more than just communicating about the trust. The trust is not an end objective. It's really more of an education and communication challenge... to teach people about the business....

> We still have a ways to go. It still gets uncomfortable when you start talking about open-book management, because our tradition has been the financial information has been very tightly controlled....

A team consisting of Gary Beil in finance, Mike Stewart in employee relations, and Peter Morton, Vice President of BCLL, has formulated a model of open-book management that reflects the connection among ownership, business competence, and openness. The model is a three-phase cycle: learning the business, running the business, and sharing the results. Beil explains,

> For example, sharing the results is more than just the ShareValue Trust—that's financial results. It is also sharing information, sharing credit. Sharing the results feeds the process of learning about the business. This is where we're getting into the open-book management concept. Giving people visibility so they understand where the business is, how it's running. So it's having business competency and having information about the business.

> And then running the business and putting all that into action. There's a connection with our performance measures and how it all fits in.

Clearly, this model represents another step by Boeing's senior management team toward coming to terms with the implications of the ShareValue Trust Program, and more broadly, Condit's Vision of 2016. This opening up is occurring at the business-unit level as well. According to Tom Schick,

> We are taking down information right to the shop floor so they see the costs and the impacts of things. A lot of the teams are interested in it. It is driven by finance support. And in some cases finance does get uncomfortable, because there are certain aspects of this thing that are very confidential. And we pick our way through it, but we will work it.

> We are not as open as we should be, but we are getting there. That's the drive. The drive is to have more and more information on the floor so that people understand the impacts and what it costs to do things. We still are very cautious, particularly when we deal with our vendor stuff and what the vendor things cost. But we are providing more and more of that going forward. Part of that is an education of the people so that they take a mature attitude toward the handling of the data. And any of the data you've given out, you're always going to expose yourself to the point that somebody is going to misuse it or abuse it or use it in ways that they shouldn't. But my philosophy, and I believe it's Phil Condit's and Ron Woodard's, is that it would be better to take a chance on having occasional problems like that but have most of the people understand the issue from a financial standpoint, than to keep everybody blind, and then ask, "Their costs are going up, what is wrong with them?" because they don't understand what the impact is. So we are doing more and more of that. We are trying to be more and more visible.

Summing Up

In telling the Boeing story, we have described the correlating changes in business strategy, firm culture, management control, and the finance role. Led by its new Chairman and CEO Phil Condit, Boeing is implementing a comprehensive set of initiatives in world-class manufacturing, financial results sharing, developing workforce business competencies, organization restructuring, and measurement systems.

These initiatives put Boeing on the path to making Condit's Vision of Boeing in 2016 a reality. Boeing has established the ShareValue Trust

Program to engage its workforce as partners in creating value for the shareholder. It is restructuring its business organization to empower its workforce. It is revamping and opening up its measurement systems to provide that workforce with the information it needs to improve process and performance.

Boeing's financial organization participates in each of these initiatives. It has played a key leadership role in the design of the ShareValue Trust Program. It is integrally involved in various operating initiatives to build the systems to support Boeing's core competency in lean manufacturing. Finance staff members are being redeployed to support the restructuring of Boeing's operating groups in small, process-focused organizations. Boeing's finance staff expects to play a key role in upgrading the financial literacy and business competencies of the firm's workforce.

Boeing executives are proud of the foregoing initiatives but are also the first to admit that they represent unfinished business. Improvements have been made in the way Boeing operates, but the jury is still out, and much work remains to be done. Complexity and culture represent formidable obstacles to change. The scope and complexity of systems improvements, such as the DCAC/MRM initiative to enable paperless airplane designs, are enormous, and the risk for failure is great. Boeing is challenging long-established cultural traits, including a command-and-control management style, highly functional mindsets, and tight control of information. Boeing is making progress, but for many, change comes hard. Some managers, both financial and nonfinancial, are finding it hard to let go of the old ways.

As the broader organization changes, the financial organization is transforming itself as well. The finance function has made the commitment to become a valued business partner. Its involvement in shaping and supporting the major business initiatives discussed in this case demonstrates that Boeing's finance organization is making this commitment a reality. This kind of influence on and involvement in the business is truly characteristic of a Business Advocate financial organization. In its focus on integrating information and staff support services, the emergence of the business resources manager concept represents the logical development of the Business Advocate model we have written about in previous research.

Finally, the Boeing case reinforces the connection between management operating philosophy and the role of the financial organization. Gary Beil notes,

> It's not just leadership in finance, it's leadership in general management, and that is as much the key to finance's role as finance leadership.... It's difficult to have a certain model and just follow through with it and say, "Well, this is the way you operate." Because change in the leaders in the various areas impacts how finance interacts and what its role is.

A financial organization cannot enact the Business Advocate role without management leadership that stresses partnership, trust, openness, and ownership of financial issues by the entire workforce. Condit's Vision of 2016 exemplifies these values.

People Interviewed

Corporate Office

Phil Condit
Chairman and CEO

Boyd Givan
Senior Vice President and CFO

Ted Collins
Senior Vice President and General Counsel

Peter Morton
Vice President, Boeing Center for Leadership and Learning

Mike Stewart
Vice President, Employee Relations

Bob Ingersoll
Merger Transition Team, Business Management

Gary Beil
Vice President and Controller

Larry Bishop
Vice President, Communications and Investor Relations

Paul Gifford
Director, Investor Relations

Curt Nohavec
Assistant Controller, Operations Planning

Sven Kalve
Senior Manager, Cost Management

Boeing Commercial Airplane Group (BCAG)

Tom Schick
Executive Vice President and Deputy to BCAG President

Gary Scott
Vice President and General Manager, 737/757 Programs

Rick Swindler
Vice President of Finance

Tom Ihrig
Director, Financial Planning

Deborah Gavin
Manager, DCAC/MRM Systems Implementation

Bob Miller
Manager, DCAC/MRM Systems Design

Defense and Space Group (D&SG)

Jerry King
Senior Vice President

Scott Carson
Senior Vice President, Business Management

Fred Whitney
Controller

Endnotes

1. Joseph F. Campbell, Jr., *Investment Report on Boeing: More Cash, Less EPS: Rocky Path to New Stock Price Highs* (Lehman Brothers, April 1996).

2. Henry A. Davis, *Cash Flow and Performance Measurement: Managing for Value* (Financial Executives Research Foundation, 1996).

3. Campbell, *Investment Report on Boeing.*

4. *ShareValue Program, A Way to Share in Our Company's Success* (Boeing, 1996).

5. *ShareValue Program.*

6

Applied Materials, Inc.[1]

Applied Materials is the world's leading supplier of semiconductor fabrication equipment, the equipment used in the production of microchips. Applied's customers read like a who's who of high technology—Hewlett Packard, Hitachi, Intel, Motorola, NEC, and Samsung, among others. Applied's products, designed by engineers and PhD scientists three organizational levels deep, make possible the microchips that are revolutionizing our world. No wonder Applied's motto is "the information age starts here."

Like other cases in this study, the Applied Materials story is one of a highly successful company in transition. But none of the other case-study firms can quite match the growth that Applied has experienced. Applied Materials is the exemplar of a financially successful high-growth, high-technology company. Over the past 20 years, Applied's sales have grown at a compound rate of 31 percent (53 percent since 1992). The 1997 *Fortune 500* rankings document Applied's outstanding financial performance during the past decade. While Applied Materials ranked 328 out of 500 with sales of $4.1 billion, it ranked first in 1986–1996 annual EPS growth rate at 76.3 percent per year. On total shareholder return for the same period, Applied was the ninth most successful, producing 40.6 percent per year. Applied has turned in this performance in the face of a notoriously cyclical business.

First and foremost, this case documents the management model Applied Materials has used to guide and govern itself over the past

---

[1] This case study contains certain forward-looking statements by Applied Materials management that are subject to risks and uncertainties that could cause actual results to differ materially from those projected. Certain of these risks and uncertainties are discussed in the company's press releases and filings with the Securities and Exchange Commission. Applied Materials assumes no obligation to update any information in this case study.

20 years. Applied has been well served by an operating philosophy, organizational culture, and management control system aligned with its strategy of growth and innovation. The Applied case is also a story of strategic transition. Applied has the goal of leading every market in which it competes. As its current markets mature, management believes that, to achieve this goal, Applied must compete on cost as well as technology. Applied has significant initiatives under way that fundamentally change the way it designs and manufactures its products. From a financial perspective, these initiatives are part of a broader initiative to nearly double the firm's revenues by the year 2000, together with making a significant improvement in its return on operating assets.

As the firm as a whole undergoes this transition, the CFO organization has its own transformation to make. In 1993, the CFO organization formulated a vision to "strategically align" its activities with its internal customers' needs. The key elements of this strategic alignment are to become more service oriented and strategically focused. The CFO organization's enunciated strategy is "to move from a transaction driven to a strategic driving organization." Given Applied's history of centralized financial control, this transition presents its own set of challenges.

Let the Story Begin

In telling the Applied case, we will alternate between stability and change—the stability and alignment of Applied's strategy, culture, and control systems and the changes Applied's management is making to reconfigure these elements to fit the company's new conditions.

The Applied Materials story will be told in terms of six themes:

1. Strategy of growth and innovation.

2. A highly entrepreneurial culture that does not tolerate financial surprises.

3. A system and structure of management control characterized by frequent operating reviews and strong financial management.

4. Transition from a business model of growth through technology innovation to a more integrated model that balances innovation and operational excellence.

5. The requisite shift in the model of management control and role of the CFO organization.

6. The challenges, tensions, and tradeoffs that confront Applied as it makes this transition.

If we cast these elements of the Applied story within the context of the conceptual framework introduced in Chapter 1, the Applied story may be visualized as shown in Figure 6.1.

The story of change at Applied covers all four bases of the model—markets, measurement, organization, and workforce, particularly management capability. The integrating mechanisms that Applied's managers stressed most in our interviews were the firm's focus on growth, its performance measurement and management review processes, and its executive compensation systems. Applied's employees participate in either a stock-option or profit-sharing program, but employee ownership did not arise as a major issue in our interviews.

FIGURE 6.1   Applied Materials: The Business Advocate Perspective—
Corporate Themes and Integrating Mechanisms

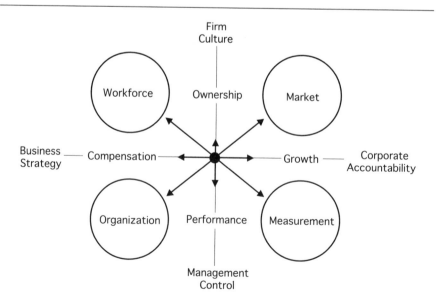

The Management Model at Applied

During Jim Morgan's 20-year tenure as Chairman and CEO, Applied Materials has followed a formula for profitable growth marked by a balanced emphasis on (1) strategic technological capability coupled with a strong focus on bringing that technology first to market and (2) a management control system designed to steer the business through rapidly changing generations of technology and business cycles. As cyclical as the chip-making equipment market is, Applied is managed for the long term in the interest of all key stakeholders. As Morgan explains,

> When I came to the company I felt that we had a set of stakeholders: shareholders, the customers, the employees, and the suppliers. So we had to have a balanced approach to the matter of creating shareholder value. But from a business decision-making viewpoint, we always had a rule that we made our decisions on what would be the long-term benefits. We insisted on maintaining a strong balance sheet so we didn't have to raise money at the wrong time. We also believe in being open with our shareholders about what we are doing. And so we have built the company based on those principles.

Guided by Morgan's balanced approach to strategy and accountability, Applied has achieved an exemplary track record of profitable growth. Over the past 20 years, sales have grown at a compound rate of 31 percent, from $22 million to approximately $4 billion. With an average return to shareholders of 40.6 percent a year over the past 10 years, shareholder value has certainly benefited from a balanced stakeholder model of accountability.

Growth Strategy: Technology and Time to Market

Above all, Applied is a technology-driven company. As Tom St. Dennis, President of the PVD Product Business Group, explains,

> In describing the importance of technology one time, Dan Maydan said to me, "Profit and revenue are like bread and water. You must have them to live. Without them you will die. But technology is like blood. You never stand the chance to make money if you don't have this."

Applied has a two-pronged growth strategy. First, in each segment in which it competes, Applied seeks to be first to market with technology that enables its customers to produce successive generations of leading-edge computer chips. The rate of change in computer chip technology is mind-boggling. Following what is referred to as Moore's Law, chip makers such as Intel have been developing a new generation every two years. Second, Applied continues to enter new segments of the chip-making equipment business. Today, Applied leads in a majority of its served markets and continues to enter new markets with the same intent. According to Paul Lindstrom, VP, Manufacturing,

> This industry is still in a high-growth period. It is still very innovative. It is not a well-established industry like automobiles where you ride the economy roller coaster up and down. That is not this industry whatsoever. You must stay on top of the technology, making the improvements along Moore's curve. You must make the improvements in your product that allow your customers, wherever they happen to be in the world, to continue down that same progression. We don't see yet a hard stop to that innovation. When that hard stop does occur, whether it's in my lifetime or not, it will become more of an operational industry at that point. Then the concern will be how you get cost out because you are not innovating every year.

It is one thing to develop or acquire technology. It is quite another thing to successfully commercialize it. The returns are high, but so are the risks. There is the cost to develop the technology coupled with the risk of missing very narrow market windows. In Applied's industry, share of market depends critically on time to market. By being first to market with enabling technologies that the Intels of this world need to bring their own products to market, a semiconductor equipment manufacturer like Applied can gain a customer's business for the duration of that generation of chips. The stakes are very high and timing is everything. Miss the technology window and you lose everything—a fact reinforced by Greg Miller, Controller, Worldwide Manufacturing Operations:

> The competitive playing field in our industry is technology and time to market. Do you have the product I need so that I can introduce the next generation microprocessor.... You've got to hit the window or you're out of the game. To a large degree, if you can hit with the right product at the right time, you can gain significant market share. When the Pentium was released, the manufacturing process for the Pentium had been decided a year before or more. If your product is ready and selected for that process or sequence of processes, you've just locked up the Pentium's whole generation. If you miss that window, you essentially have to wait for the next generation of chips for your next opportunity.

Tom St. Dennis talked about the current challenges of making the transition to the new 12-inch wafer technology:

To me, the challenges today are still time-to-market issues and technology. This is compounded by the wafer size change that our industry is going to go through. It's going from eight inch to twelve inch. That investment in RD&E [research, development, and engineering] will probably get close to $100 million. It's a whole new generation of systems.... But as I have tried to remind everyone in the company, it's more than just a bigger wafer, it's also much more sophisticated technology. It's also going to be the system that the next three generations of Intel microprocessors will be built on.... And Applied Materials is going to generate an additional $50 to $100 billion in revenue out of this product platform over the next ten years.

Performance Measurement: Customers, Market Share, and Margins

Because Applied is populated by scientists and engineers, it should be no surprise that the company has a highly measurement-oriented culture. The incentive system is objective and formula driven. The performance measurement system places equal weight on both operational and financial metrics. The computation of annual bonuses is based on a multiplicative relationship between these two sets of measures. Thus, poor performance on either set reduces the total bonus payout. A case in point is the measurement system for the CVD Product Business Group, as explained by Managing Director Dave Fried:

> What constitutes success for me is very simple: market share, profitability, and quality. We have specific market share goals. To achieve these goals, I need to be growing.... And we know exactly that if we meet x percent, we get y payout. Profitability is the same thing. The measurement is very straightforward. If your profitability is x, you get y payout. We are measured on three things: gross margin, net income before taxes and interest expense, and return on operating assets.... The third criterion of success is quality, which is measured by on-time delivery, customer satisfaction based on some external surveys we do with our customers, and cost of ownership.

The performance measurement system reflects Applied's strategy of technology and time-to-market. When we asked Fried what the superordinate goal was, he did not hesitate to respond:

> Market share. If you woke up anybody in CVD in the middle of the night and said, "What's the most important thing in your life?" they'd say, "Market share." It's market share because that's what our executives emphasize. The thinking has been, if you get market share, we'll figure out how to get the necessary financial performance. But if you don't have the market share, you will not have the chance to go work on your financial performance.

Jerry Taylor, CFO, confirmed that, "Executives get called on the carpet if they have product portfolio or market share issues."

As part of a strategic transition under way at Applied, senior management has recently changed the weightings in the performance measurement system to focus greater managerial attention on asset management. But before we move on to the strategic transition that Applied is making, let's consider the second half of Morgan's business model—disciplined management control.

"No-Surprises" Management Control

The challenges of profitable growth extend beyond technological leadership and market share. In a highly uncertain environment of technological change and steep swings in business cycle, profitability can be elusive. Applied has established a highly disciplined management control system designed to contain the chaos and avoid the financial surprises that come from rapid commercialization.

Jim Morgan discussed the importance he placed on financial management from the very start. As a counterbalance to the unavoidable uncertainty of the marketplace, he has consciously focused on building an infrastructure of financial control that stresses predictability and avoiding financial surprise. He explains,

> The financial management system is something I tried to get in early. So it's kind of a given. It's predictable. It's right. It's timely. We don't wake up to find that we have a bunch of inventory we don't have reserves for—the basic kind of stuff that companies in high tech tend to get bogged down in because they don't pay any attention to it. And they don't get the infrastructure in place for doing it right.

> And so we have been fortunate to get that in place. And it's been consistently of enough quality that we've been able to deliver all the time. If you talk to the Street, the Street doesn't know if our business is going to go up or down, because we don't know, but they know that we will manage our business effectively in a slowdown and that the decisions will be made to assure success for the long term.

If there is a core principle underlying Applied's approach to management control, it would be the principle of "no surprises." In discussing the fiduciary role of the CFO and his commitment to a strong financial function, Jim Morgan reported with pride that there have been no major financial surprises on his watch as Chairman and CEO. Morgan said,

From a financial integrity viewpoint, the CFO has access to the board. And that's by design. There's effort periodically to subjugate finance into some other role than that. We assign controllers to units. I make it very clear that the business-unit controllers, wherever they are in the world, report to the CFO.... So we've had that, and it has worked pretty well in our company. Some of the people chafe at it a little bit, but it's never gotten out of hand. So far it's worked quite well. So far we've never had a surprise in my 20 years. And that's an important part.

The CEO's expectation of no financial surprises constitutes a core tenet of Applied's management culture. In our interviews, the expectation came up time and again as a taken-for-granted principle of Applied's management control philosophy. Jerry Taylor, CFO, is justifiably proud of Applied's track record of profitable growth and the contribution that his financial organization has made. Taylor said,

This business is not a U.S. industry. This is a global industry. You have to be a global player. And we do it pretty well without tax surprises, without treasury surprises, without foreign exchange surprises, without accounting surprises. This doesn't mean our business results don't change. We're out at the forefront of making them change for the better. And it's not done with mirrors. It's done with good people working their butts off.

We do all this, and we avoid financial surprises. We do it because we work well with operations and we have an oversight responsibility that we know how to perform as well. The operating people are charged with driving this business very dynamically. The growth in the enterprise of over $3 billion in the past three years doesn't get much faster, particularly the fact that 65 percent of the revenue growth is outside of the United States.

Line managers are quickly acculturated to this expectation. Tom St. Dennis has been with Applied for about five years. In discussing Applied's financial review process, Tom referred to the principle of no surprises:

In regard to the financial review process ... with Morgan, I know it's no surprises. He talks about it and he's proud of it. I'm not getting my job done if there are surprises. The process is well supported through our financial review process. It's not like I wake up every day and have to worry, "Is there a surprise today that I ought to be thinking about?"

The support Tom St. Dennis refers to are the two cornerstones of Applied's no-surprises management control system: (1) an uncompromising demand for financial integrity championed through the fiduciary role and functional strength of the CFO organization and (2) an intensive management review process that forecasts, evaluates, and resizes the business on a quarterly basis.

Strong CFO Organization

Conservative financial management and a strong focus on the fiduciary role of the finance organization have been the counterbalance to the no-holds-barred entrepreneurialism that Morgan has encouraged on the business side. He noted,

> I've always been a strong supporter of finance as a functional strength at a time, particularly in Silicon Valley, when financial people were treated as bean counters. They didn't participate much in things. That really defined the start of us. One of the early things I did was to put in a good financial system. I got a new controller. The financial department has always had full access to everything that goes on in the company. That's just the rule.

Greg Miller, Controller of Worldwide Manufacturing Operations, offered his view of the relationship between Morgan's philosophy of no surprises and his expectation of the finance organization:

> Jim Morgan says that we [finance] can be everything else we want to be as long as we control the business and ensure predictable results—consistent predictable results. How do you get that? I want a strong controller function. I don't want surprises. We're in a cyclical industry, but I want our internal processes and controls to be such that in the short term we don't miss our guidance to Wall Street.

To ensure the unassailable integrity of the information used by management to operate the business and the information shared with Wall Street, Morgan has insisted on a strong, centrally managed CFO organization. Business-unit controllers are physically decentralized and participate as part of the business-unit teams but maintain their primary allegiance and "hard-line" reporting relationship to the CFO. In a company with a highly entrepreneurial culture in which line managers are given the freedom to run their business, this hard-line relationship of the business-unit controllers to the CFO has not gone unchallenged. But Morgan has stood firm. Steve Newberry, former Group VP and member of the firm's six-person Executive Committee, commented about this in discussing the role that finance has played:

> Morgan made it very clear many years ago that this is a highly entrepreneurial company but that financial integrity and conservatism were absolute requirements. Therefore, when Jerry Taylor came in the early 1980s, he

was able to achieve a level of control and compliance to policies, because when they were deviated from, finance would go to war. And if it ever got escalated all the way to the top, it was no question, Morgan backed finance every single time.... So that battle was over and done with a long time ago. People still test it from time to time, but they lose every time.

In recent years, under the leadership of Jerry Taylor, Applied's finance organization has sought to enhance its business partner role. In doing so, Morgan has reminded finance not to forget Job Number One. According to Mike O'Farrell, VP and Corporate Controller,

> Our chairman has always been very strong on the fiduciary role of finance and that it's their role to speak up. They don't have a secondary allegiance. Obviously they are concerned about the success of their own business unit, but he expects the finance people to be able to go into any meeting and escalate as necessary any financial issues or exposures, and that's Job One for finance.

> So it's interesting. When we were developing our vision and mission statements, we put that as our number one mission.... And Jim reinforced that on his end—that that is our number one job. If you don't have the financial integrity in the numbers that finance brings forth, you don't have the opportunity to partner, because if people are quibbling that the numbers are wrong or they're all screwed up or whatever, you're not a business partner at that point. Instead, you're just always trying to perfect or refine the numbers. So you have to have that almost impeccable profile and that financial integrity to be invited in as a true business partner. If everything in your shop is clean and working well and you are presenting the company with the right issues and the right numbers and over and above that you can add value in terms of how we look at the business, then OK.

Management Review Process:
Running a Long-Term Business a Quarter at a Time

Applied's management control philosophy is to counterbalance its aggressive entrepreneurialism with a very disciplined management infrastructure of business planning and review. Applied devotes a tremendous amount of management time and attention to the operating review process. And nobody questions the value of this process. There is very strong commitment to this process throughout the ranks of management. Jim Morgan explains,

> We worry about the accuracy of everything that we do. But a lot of companies will review very carefully the actual performance against the annual

operating plan. We look at that, but most of the discussion is against the forecast, and the forecast is done on a 12-month rolling basis, at least every quarter, in a serious way. It's also done every month. We do a roll-up forecast from the bottom up.

But we really plan the business on a quarterly basis. So we try to focus on getting enough bookings to fill up a quarter and a half. Then we'll raise our cost structure or slow it down depending on what the forecast is beyond the period.... We run a long-term business a quarter at a time.

Steve Newberry is responsible for the firm's business planning process and operating results. Every quarter the top 30 corporate and business-unit executives meet for a three- to five-day review. Two other times a month, Newberry meets with individual business-unit management teams. He said,

I meet with these executives in three different types of meetings a quarter. One, they have a quarterly operations review where they commit for the quarter and a rolling four-quarter forecast. Then about six weeks later, they update in what we call a quarterly forecast review. Where are they against their commitment? And how are they doing? Then in the middle of the quarter, we have a quarterly business review. The emphasis is not financial. It's on what is happening in the business. But in that meeting, they do update their financials.

Mostly we have a contextual discussion. What are customers spending on? How are we doing competitively? I share with them where the corporation is and how I feel about their performance. Then I put my concerns and issues on the table and we have a dialogue. Morgan and Maydan get their shot at whatever they want to position. It's part of how we express our expectations as a senior management group. It's part of how the business-unit executives express their concerns and issues back to us. These are pretty dynamic meetings. The quarterly business review is a three- to five-day event. If it's five, it usually has some training in it. The top 30 executives participate.

Some of the business-unit managers we interviewed commented on the management review process. Tom St. Dennis said, "We resize our business every month, and we replan our business every quarter.... And in a business that changes as fast as our business changes, checking the size every month is okay with me."

The management review process at the business-unit level cascades through all levels of the firm. As Greg Miller explained,

There's a fairly extensive review process in this company. Every business unit every month has a business review with the corporate executives—and that has been a constant for the 12 years I've been here. This has never, ever, changed—every single month for 12 years.

Each business unit conducts its own internal operational reviews at every level. Every unit within a division conducts an operations review every month. And what people are going after are the business fundamentals. They're looking at their spending; they're looking at the programs and projects. They've got performance metrics that they're measuring to. There's a lot of review and checking in this company that takes the place of prevention through good, stable, mature business processes. Since we don't have a high level of process maturity, we do a lot of checking and review. It's necessary and it works.

The Balance-Sheet Review Process: Avoiding Financial Surprises

The balance-sheet review process epitomizes the disciplined character of Applied's approach to management control. First, it illustrates very concretely how Applied's management control system operates to avoid financial surprises. Second, it illustrates the traditional role the financial organization has played as the champion of financial integrity. Third, recent changes in the balance-sheet review process exemplify senior management's efforts to make the business units more accountable for asset management. Historically, the balance-sheet review process has been "owned" by finance. In recent years, Applied's financial organization has taken the initiative to integrate balance-sheet management more fully into business operations. This initiative to share ownership with line managers exemplifies the CFO organization's drive to develop its role as a business partner.

The balance-sheet review at Applied has a history. To keep business-unit managers focused on its strategy of technology and time to market, Applied's senior management team has made them accountable for achieving two primary targets: market share and profit contribution. This focus is clearly reflected in Applied's performance measurement and incentive systems.

With business-unit attention focused on market share and profit contribution, the corporate office historically has managed the balance sheet.

Steve Newberry commented on the reliance on centralized asset management at Applied:

> Historically, balance-sheet and asset management at the business-unit level has been weak in terms of accountability because the way the company got asset turns was by leveraging the net income side of the equation. Asset management wasn't highly incentivized relative to market share and to gross margin. And so in the business units, you really had the finance organization watching the balance sheet.
>
> Now there were exceptions, because the head of operations or the head of the group was concerned about asset management. But at the corporate level, between Bagley [former COO] and Taylor [CFO], they watched that side of the equation. They, in turn, expected the finance group to bring the analysis, the implications, the issues.

One of the primary means employed by finance staff to support senior management is the balance-sheet review. Mike O'Farrell noted,

> To ensure financial integrity, we primarily utilize the balance sheet review process. This financial review process utilizes a balance sheet orientation. If the reserve or liability appears on the balance sheet, the business units have stepped up to it. If they haven't, it's off books, and it hasn't hit the P&L. So it is similar to what public accounting firms use in their audit process, with the focus on a balance sheet review to ensure financial integrity. But in our process we also talk about issues, trends, opportunities and coordination items that we need to be aware of from the P&L perspective.

Over the years, the balance-sheet review process has become highly developed and provides the CFO organization with insight into and foresight about the business so that financial surprises can be avoided. Business issues and risks are identified. Every quarter at the business-unit level, each balance-sheet account is reconciled and all known liabilities are accrued and reserved for. Unresolved balances must be identified and plans established to resolve discrepancies. For example, installation and warranty costs as well as obsolete inventory are significant issues to manage in Applied's business. When the objective is to deliver leading-edge solutions for a customer under a short time fuse, a delivered product may require intensive installation and servicing support. Forecasting these costs is not an exact science. Applied has used the balance-sheet review process to regularly revisit, and revise as necessary, the costs the company expects to incur and to identify and head off emerging problems caused by poor operational management in these areas.

A broader self-assessment of internal controls is conducted annually by each business unit and is folded into the quarterly balance-sheet review process. The self-assessment covers internal controls, best practices, and company policies and methodologies as they relate to operational areas and business processes (e.g., inventory management, procurement, and cash disbursement process). All policies and self-assessment questionnaires are online. No matter where they are around the globe, business-unit personnel conducting the review can submit questions about policies, practices, and accounting guidance via e-mail to the corporate office. The corporate office, in turn, has targeted a goal of responding to any questions within 48 hours.

Shared Ownership of a Business-Oriented Balance-Sheet Review

Finance has come to realize that the fundamental issue in the balance-sheet review process is ownership by line management. As long as the process was perceived as being owned by finance, line managers were not integrally involved. Issues would be identified, but getting line management to follow through on action items was often problematic. Jerry Taylor explained, "In the finance function there's always the issue of how we get the operating unit to go fix what we have identified as a deficiency. Because most of this stuff is who owns it...."

Mike O'Farrell discussed this problem and his belief that the balance-sheet review process must be jointly owned by finance and line management. He said,

> We felt that the self-assessment was largely ending in the finance forum. And we also had a balance-sheet review process that was largely a group of finance people—the worldwide operations controller, the corporate controller, the individual business-unit controllers—sitting around the table, all critiquing their numbers. Our feeling was that we had a disciplined process but we didn't have the right players to get full value from this process.
>
> So we went back to the business-unit GMs [general managers] and said we would like this to be a healthier process. We'd like the balance-sheet reviews to be run by the business-unit executive head or their number two guy. The GM will bring his procurement and marketing directors, his manufacturing director, his field service director, and we'll go through the balance-sheet review. But then we'll step back from the numbers and figure out what operational activities are causing the numbers to be a problem or

a positive. We'll root-cause the issue.... Why are we scrapping so much material? Why aren't we screening our purchasing better for demand or engineering changes? We look back at the drivers. We try to identify the issues that might allow us to improve our financial performance and/or reduce our risks.

Dissatisfaction with the lack of ownership of the balance-sheet review process by the line was not restricted to finance. As the former executive in charge of business planning and operational financial performance, Steve Newberry shared his philosophy that ultimately balance-sheet issues are line-management issues:

> I have insisted that finance needs to lead the process of transferring the ownership because they have had it and it's not acceptable to me. I won't let a finance executive get up and talk about the P&L. Why do I want finance executive to get up and talk about a balance sheet? Who creates the pluses and minuses on that thing? The line does. So since that's not what occurred, they've got to go and transfer that. So we've got an education process in place to do that.

The same sentiment was expressed at the business-unit level. Dave Fried, a former finance executive and now Managing Director of the CVD Product Business Group, observed that the balance-sheet review process had been limited to participation of finance staff in spite of its relevance to business operations:

> It used to be different. It used to be just finance to finance. So the controller would go and present to Mike O'Farrell and say, "Here's what's happening in my division." And nobody from operations would be there. Mike O'Farrell and Mercedes Johnson, the Corporate Controller and the former Operations Controller, changed that about a year and a half ago. The balance-sheet review involves issues related to receivables, excess and obsolete inventory, and installation and warranty reserves. But the importance is very big because installation and warranty really drive a bunch of operational issues.

Line ownership of the balance-sheet review process is strengthened by the requirement that business-unit GMs report key results of the review in their quarterly business review with Newberry and other senior corporate executives. O'Farrell said,

> Steve Newberry added a requirement that each business executive review their 'A' category of internal control weaknesses on a quarterly basis with him and with Executive Committee members in the room. So everyone sees what the big business issues are that have been identified relative to internal control weaknesses and opportunities and any policy deviations. If the

issues are global in scope, then they also address that as a management team.

With that kind of mandate and support of top management, the role of finance in this process has shifted from pure oversight of line operations to partnership with line personnel to aid them in their self-assessment. O'Farrell continued,

> We moved the focus away from just finance people doing this activity. We have involved the operational people in doing the self-assessment. But the key is who really owns the output into operational forums. Business-unit managers own the balance-sheet review activity as well as the self-assessment activity. I think that is a positive. We've turned the hat around a little bit here and said, finance is not the police and implementers. We are facilitators in this process, and we'll work with operations to get it done. It is a collaborative process with operations to make improvements in the company's business processes and controls. I believe that this process served the company well during the recent industry downturn.

Dave Fried concurred when we asked him about the value of the balance-sheet review process:

> We make sure that the operational people in the balance-sheet reviews understand what is going on. So I think that's a really good process because it puts the connection between what's on the balance sheet and what actions did you take to cause either these good things to happen or these bad things to happen. So you wrote a whole bunch of engineering changes to change the product to get all these great cost reductions. But did you also put in immediate effectivity so that now we're throwing away $2 million? You just wiped out your benefit. So we're trying to put those feedback loops in.

> When we go do our balance-sheet reviews it's the operations people from each division, but primarily to me. So they're presenting to me at the meeting that we're following GAAP and there are no fiduciary issues. But it's really an operational review with finance.

The transfer of ownership of balance-sheet review has resulted in a much healthier and more effective management review process. By approaching the balance-sheet review as a jointly owned, business-oriented process, Applied's finance organization has played an important role in transforming the process from one focused on avoiding financial surprises to one that also plays a major role in improving business operations. Finance provides guidance in establishing and ensuring the integrity of the process. Line management owns the process and is responsible for the action items and the improvements that should result. The balance-sheet review has also established an important element of the management infrastructure required to support Applied's transition to a new management model and its initiative in strategic asset management.

Strategic Transition

The management model just described has served Applied Materials very well over the past 20 years. The firm's documented record of growth in revenues, market share, profits, and shareholder wealth attests to this. But the markets in which Applied competes show signs of maturing. As its markets mature, senior management is readying Applied to compete on cost as well as technology. Competing on cost requires that Applied focus on operational excellence with the fervor it has brought to commercializing its technology. This shift from a focus on innovation to a dual focus on both technology innovation and operational excellence represents a major strategic transition for Applied.

In addition to the external stimulus of market maturation, an internal stimulus drives strategic change in Applied's management model. With leadership and support from the finance organization, senior management is focusing on more aggressive asset management. Managers at Applied have concluded that there is more leverage to improve profitability through aggressive asset management than through margin management, especially if margins do come under increasing pressure as markets mature.

In emphasizing asset management, senior management is not backing away from its growth strategy. Rather, senior management believes business-unit management capability has matured to the point where it can pursue growth, operational excellence, and efficient asset utilization simultaneously. Going forward, Applied has set even more ambitious growth and profitability goals than those it has achieved in the past. In 1996, Applied Materials had $4.1 billion in sales with a return on operating assets (ROOPA) of 28.7 percent. Its goal is to exceed $8 billion in sales by 2000, together with a significant improvement in ROOPA. The company's longer term goal is to get its ROOPA to 44 percent. In view of these goals, we think it's fair to say that Applied's highly entrepreneurial, achievement-oriented management culture is clearly intact.

Like the firm, the CFO organization has a transformation to make. The CFO organization seeks to strategically align its mission with its internal customers' needs. The key elements of this strategic alignment are becoming more service oriented and strategically focused. The CFO organization's enunciated strategy is, "to move from a transaction-driven to a strategic-driving organization." Given Applied's history of centralized financial control, this transition presents its own set of challenges. In the remainder of this case, we discuss the strategic transition occurring in the firm and the finance function.

Market Change and Organization Change

High-growth companies like Applied Materials often make strategic tradeoffs. One such tradeoff is between technological innovation and operational excellence. Competing in an environment of rapid technological change and tight market windows takes tremendous focus. Technology and time to market are the all-consuming priorities. Other aspects of the business are often sacrificed to these higher priorities. Paul Lindstrom, VP, Manufacturing, explained,

> The engineer is here to say, "I deal with technology. I'm a creative person. I have to innovate. I have to get to the next level of technology. Do not get in my way. Do not encumber me with concurrent engineering requirements to get the right manufacturing shape so we assemble it from the top instead of the front and make sure the thing can go together only one way." They don't necessarily worry about those serviceability and manufacturability issues. They are worried about getting the performance out of the product, first and foremost.

Julio Aranovich is the executive in charge of Worldwide Manufacturing Operations (WMO) and is Paul Lindstrom's boss. As head of WMO, Julio is responsible for all common manufacturing modules, which account for 70 percent of Applied's manufacturing activity, and for materials management worldwide. Julio holds a doctorate in physics. His two previous jobs were on the product side of the business. Consequently, Julio can speak to both the technology and manufacturing sides of Applied. He talked about the tension between technology and manufacturing:

> Applied is a technology company, which causes problems and frustrations in trying to manage the manufacturing organization. The tension exists in

every single company in the world. It's one of typical tensions: R&D and operations. Every three, four years, corporations reorganize with a new response. The question is not whether there is a tension. The question is, "Is the tension more acute in our case or a different manifestation?" And a little bit it is.

I have worked for two other companies. These other companies were much more structured and therefore were much more balanced between manufacturing and technology. Why are they more balanced than we are? I believe it is because we do not sell to end consumers. We do not sell commodities. We sell enabling equipment—equipment that enables you to do things that hopefully others can't do. Then technology content is essential and everything else tends to be secondary.

But many managers at Applied believe that trading off innovation for operational excellence in manufacturing is no longer viable. Why? Partly because the product and the industry are maturing, and partly because the customer is becoming more demanding. Senior management believes that it must now compete with equal vigor on both dimensions. Aranovich offered his view as to why Applied's historical emphasis on technology over manufacturing is no longer viable:

When I began in the semiconductor industry, if you got 10 percent yield from your first runs, you were okay. Then you worked your butt off, and you'd get it to be 50 percent. Today, some of my customers in the Far East run their dynamic RAM lines at 95 percent yield. This is unbelievable, if you think about it. This is a sequence of theoretically almost impossible events, 500 of them in a row. And the total yield is a multiplication. It's the worst possible case from a mathematical point of view. And yet at the end after you multiply the yield of the one stage by the yield of the next, you still get 90-something percent.

But our customers are hitting diminishing returns in this process. They are now saying, "Let's look at the next guy for further improvement, the equipment manufacturer. The way to reduce costs is to make you, the equipment manufacturer, do more things than you used to do, in addition to enabling us to move technology forward." So the equation is changing.... We have come from where manufacturing was practically unimportant to where it is one of the most important competencies to have, and we are in the transition period.

Steve Newberry made a similar point:

The customer's requirements keep going up and up and up in terms of what he is willing to accept in terms of the maturity level of that product. This means if you don't change your engineering process, if you don't

change your market requirements generation process, and if you don't change
your definition of success and you keep operating to the old methodology,
you're going to start having some real problems.... You're vulnerable to
being leap-frogged. And you see that.

As Newberry's and Aranovich's comments indicate, Applied's executive management team believes that the semiconductor manufacturing industry, like other industries, will follow a predictable path of
evolution through the stages of innovation, differentiation, and cost competition. As its industry matures, management believes Applied will not
be able to compete solely on its leading-edge technology. In fact, this
has already happened. Applied has differentiated its product line, and
in those product lines, the more mature technologies are increasingly
competitive. As Ron Foster, Controller of Etch Product Business Group,
explained,

> Etch is in it. We're neck deep in it. We've got a third of the market. Lam has
> a third of the market. Tokyo Electron has a third of the market. We're in a
> very competitive situation. Technological functionality has to be there, but
> price also has to be there. I can't negotiate beyond certain levels, and we
> lose deals on price. The PVD business group doesn't as much, but we
> do.... It's the normal maturation of the industry that's going on.

Foster elaborated on the impact on how the Etch business is now
being managed. In response to our question as to whether the Etch
managers are stressing the cost side of the business, he responded,

> Absolutely. Joe Bronson [GM] is telling them, "You need this gross margin.
> That translates to this cost. Get it done, and we can't wait three years after
> introduction to be there." But it's not just cost. It's the whole pricing-margin
> equation. So we instituted a margin management process starting with pre-
> quote to the customer, which we've never done before. Now we have
> quote management meetings in each one of the divisions. The controller
> facilitates it.

Operational Excellence

Competing on price as well as technology requires more than margin
management meetings. It requires a focus on operational excellence
that Applied has not had in the past. Applied's management believes
that if the firm is to continue to grow profitably, it must develop the
business and management infrastructure that will enable it to pursue
technological superiority and operational excellence simultaneously.

When we asked Steve Newberry about this joint imperative, he echoed Julio Aranovich's belief that Applied is now in a period of strategic transition:

> You have gotten right into the middle of what is the major strategic issue in this company. This company is in transition. We're trying to move from being largely entrepreneurial and in many areas relatively undisciplined—fortunately not in financial policies and procedures—to a vision of what we call a big, fast, global competitor. This means entrepreneurial and disciplined. You have to stop thinking in terms of, "If you're disciplined, you're not entrepreneurial; if you're entrepreneurial, you're not disciplined." You have to be both. You want individual excellence, and you want teamwork. And you want enabling business processes as a vehicle as opposed to the chaos that occurs if you don't have any of this stuff right.

Newberry's comment about the need to be both entrepreneurial and disciplined is key. Operational excellence is necessary not only in order to compete on price. It is equally important to Applied's continued ability to innovate. Even as part of Applied's business matures, it must continue to create leading-edge products. Tom St. Dennis pointed out that failure to execute operationally can hamper Applied's ability to continue to do what has made it so successful—commercializing innovative technology. He said,

> All of our businesses are becoming extended over various segments of the product life cycle. All of us have got some older products that are sustaining kinds of things and maybe some sunset products. Yet, at the other end, it is the most competitive environment in our industry. Back here we generate a lot of margin and revenue, and out there it's all a design win kind of thinking.... So the organization has to cover a very broad spectrum of products.

> The older products can really slow you down. If your quality isn't right, if your cost isn't right, if your customer support isn't right, if your infrastructure isn't right, you get so internally focused back on these things that you start to lose it out at the front end.... But the only way to make it a no-brainer is to do it right up front. It's real front-end loaded on the investment side. You have to get it documented well. You have to get it tested well. Then you have to get it launched into a manufacturing process that's stable and cost effective.

Process-Focused Organization:
The Capability and Discipline of Operational Excellence

Depending on who you talk to and where they have their finger on the elephant, Applied has any number of initiatives under way to build the business process infrastructure of operational excellence—lean manufacturing, supply chain management, concurrent engineering, product option architecture, and so on. Whatever the name, what is clear is that, much like Boeing, Applied is trying to recreate itself into a process-focused organization. As Steve Newberry noted,

> What you find is that people are describing the elephant to you and one's at the trunk and one's at the tail.... A couple of years ago, we started with order fulfillment. We said the order fulfillment process is from quote to sign-off. And it's made up of a whole set of processes that need to be developed or reengineered or created. You need product-option architecture as a fundamental architecture for engineering configuration. You have the product-specification tool. Then you have the lean manufacturing initiative, because you can also call this whole thing the lean production system. So we have had so many of these initiatives going off, not totally coordinated.... But we're bringing that back in.

The complexity of the change is great, but so is the financial opportunity. For instance, Jerry Taylor described the firm's initiative to reengineer the way product configurations are engineered and sold:

> Take our Model 5000 system. We're not talking about what goes on in the process chamber, which is the heart of our business. We're talking about all the other stuff that is hung around the system, such as where the power signal lights go and so on. There are 40,000 combinations just in one system on one product line, and we do this manually.

> We're trying to move to a product-option architecture that says, if you select this option architecture, you can generate a bill of materials that can be buildable on the factory floor. Today we configure this as well as we can, but we still get major changes on the factory floor. This combination doesn't fit with that combination. We don't do poorly at it, and we have cut our cycle times. But we want to cut our cycle times dramatically in the next three years using the lean manufacturing and the lean procurement concepts to give us a real competitive advantage.

> This initiative hooks up dramatically to asset management. If we deploy this product-option architecture initiative right, out of a current balance sheet of $4 billion to $5 billion, we can harvest $1 billion in cash over the next five years.

The Organizational and Cultural Challenge

Despite the complexity involved, possibly the greatest challenge that Applied faces in becoming more process focused is its own past success as a technology company. The challenge is to gain the attention and commitment of engineers who have been trained to focus on technology and time to market, and the business-unit entrepreneurs who have been rewarded for driving the success of their specific products. Historically, the product business units have functioned largely independent of one another and have been masters of their own destiny. A process-focused organization requires common disciplines and coordination from the engineering and manufacturing of the product through its delivery to the customer. For the product business units that have treated manufacturing as an afterthought, this represents a fundamental organizational and cultural change.

The person who faces this challenge day in and day out is Paul Lindstrom, VP of Manufacturing. Although he is in charge of manufacturing, Lindstrom is painfully aware that how the product is developed and released is critical to any effort to implement a lean production system. He said,

> My agenda is to reengineer manufacturing for Applied Materials. I must get the attention of product general managers and the Executive Committee. Manufacturing is not one large entity. It is segmented. There is a common part of the product, which is the organization that I have.

> The second half of the manufacturing is within the product groups. I am a supplier to them of common platforms on which they put their process chambers. And then they ship them. But the manufacturing strategies are not just manufacturing in nature. They are operational in nature. They are process oriented. They make fundamental changes in how Applied Materials must behave to allow a lot of these rewards to come to reality. That's where the cultural piece and the organizational piece can get in the way.

One would think that the transition to common engineering processes would be relatively straightforward for a high-technology company populated by engineers. Not so, says Steve Newberry, himself an engineer:

> Where do you start? There's no question you need to start with how you engineer products. You need to change how you engineer them. Because if they're not designed to be configurable and optionable and testable, they can't be sold that way.

Why is it taking so long? Because engineering does not exist in this company. Technology does, and that's a big difference. This is a technology company, not an engineering company. They may call themselves engineers, but they do not practice like engineers. And if they came here and they were good engineers, they didn't stay very long because you weren't allowed to be a good engineer. You had to get to market. You had to innovate quickly. And if you needed more time, no. You don't get more time. You do it now.

Performance Measurement as a Lever of Change

In this world ruled by enabling technology and time to market, the definition of success has been "results on the wafer." Engineers have focused on that, for which the firm and they have been richly rewarded. Newberry continued,

> Well, that used to be the definition of success because you didn't need to have a higher level of success. In this business if you could get a result on the wafer with a minimum amount of reliability and running cost of ownership, you could win. We clearly proved that. Because that's what this company was all about—technologically superior results on the wafer. And we supported the hell out of it. We did whatever it took.

As customer demands have grown from enabling technology to cost of ownership, and as Applied looks to grow its own profitability through more efficient operations and use of assets, results on the wafer to the exclusion of other definitions of success are no longer acceptable. Newberry explained,

> Lean manufacturing... includes a whole set of requirements, including engineering specifications for product that is designed for serviceability and designed for manufacturability, so that manufacturing can now define the sequence of events within the factory that are going to enable a lean line to exist. It requires documentation and capability so that the suppliers can be a successful part of the JIT [just-in-time] deliveries so that the whole kanban system works. It requires that customer orders from marketing, either for an optioned configurable system or for a customized order, are all done in ways that are in sync with a recognized strategy of total cost, total cycle time, and total quality relative to the delivered product.

> Now what does it take to get that? What is the organization's fundamental definition of success? Is it, "I'm successful in engineering if I am time-to-market successful with a new capability despite the fact that it missed its cost target by 150 percent, the fact that it's not reliable enough yet, or that

its quality is not consistently achievable because my design is not manufacturable or documentable?"

Senior management is using the incentive program and performance measurement system as the primary lever to change that definition of success. It has put its money where its mouth is by clearly linking its operational improvement initiatives to the firm's financial performance and executive compensation plans. Earlier we referred to the ambitious objectives Applied has set to improve its return on operating assets, with a longer term objective of 44 percent. It has set aggressive financial targets that it believes cannot be achieved without achieving these initiatives.

According to Newberry, the only way Applied's management team can hit this target is to change the way Applied does business by successfully implementing its process-improvement initiatives. If this change is achieved, executives and shareholders stand to benefit substantially. He said,

> Now if you look at where a group is and you put them up against that definition of success, the group looks and says, "We have a problem." Now either they are not going to believe that it's achievable or they will realize they need a strategy. What's the strategy? The strategy is that we have to design our products differently. We must market them differently. We must manufacture them differently.

> And if we do, what does that look like? It looks like products that have this kind of design-to-cost parameter. That they will be engineered with this kind of modularity and testability from the start. And all of us will be rewarded not in terms of what your little incremental contribution is. Part of your reward may be based on that, but it's a small part. It's whether collectively we reach these levels of success. And we can't get there unless everybody plays in the game to that common definition.

Strategic Asset Management:
The Integrating Link Between Operational Excellence and Profitability

As Steve Newberry's comments suggest, senior management believes that process improvement can significantly boost the company's ROA. To put teeth in this assertion, they are tying executive compensation to this linkage.

With leadership and support from Jerry Taylor's staff, senior management has launched a major initiative, which it calls strategic asset management, to look at the firm-wide opportunity to improve asset utilization through major process improvements. Nancy Handel, Vice President, Corporate Finance, and Treasurer, is the leader within finance on this initiative. She talked about the broader stakes involved:

> From a financial perspective, we are targeting peak profitability for this company in an upturn at 20 percent after tax…. In our best of times we did close to 17 percent. The most we can improve if we get to the peak is 3 percent of sales. The question then is, what are those tools and what is available to differentiate Applied Materials in terms of value to the equity shareholder, value to the employees? Well, it has to do with the next area we can go after, the asset base.

Based on a benchmarking study conducted on its behalf by a major consulting firm and the assessment of the balance-sheet improvements resulting from its planned business process improvements, Applied managers believe asset management offers significant leverage to improve the profitability of the firm, especially compared with its historical focus on margin management. According to Mike O'Farrell,

> We benchmarked several areas, and we were ranked first in our industry on one out of several metrics. We were much farther down in others. So we said, okay, if we either do what we used to be able to do or match our competition on these other metrics, we could create another $3 billion in cash. Whereas if we improve profitability, even to the peak target, we only get about $1 billion. So the asset side gives you a 3-to-1 leverage…. That's $3 billion less of capital we have to raise through issuing stock…. Everyone benefits. Our outside shareholders benefit, our inside shareholders benefit, the employees benefit through profit sharing.

The Management Infrastructure of Asset Management

Applied's senior management is establishing a management infrastructure to promote achievement of its ROA targets and the operational excellence initiatives discussed earlier. This infrastructure institutes fundamental change in the firm's organizational governance, its performance measurement systems, its capital budgeting process, and its management culture and capability.

First, senior management is decentralizing accountability for asset management to the business-unit level. While acknowledging this change, Jim Morgan was also careful to point out that Applied must not forget its primary focus on technology and the customer:

> We're trying to make product groups more accountable for their asset management. And so their incentives are based on asset turns. There's been a lot more emphasis on that in the last two to three years. In our business, if we get the right product, the rest of it doesn't matter. I mean it does, you have to do it reasonably well, but first things first. If you get too focused on asset management, you can't meet a customer's ramp. One advantage is that we're at the heart of a customer's business. That means they really want us as a partner and they do a lot to nurture our success. On the other hand, we're right at the heart of their business. If there is a screw-up, it doesn't take very long to get to me. And so the priority is customer, product, and then good asset management.

As accountability for asset management is pushed down to the business units, the performance measurement system is changing. Historically, asset management at the business-unit level has placed a distant third to sales growth and margin management. Applied has driven its returns through above-the-line growth in sales. By being first to market with enabling technologies required by its customers, Applied has been able to earn very healthy margins.

Apart from intensive balance-sheet management during downturns, senior management's concern has been to make sure sufficient assets were in place to support the company's growth. Nancy Handel discussed the change required. Talking about the need to shift business-unit managers' P&L orientation to an ROA mentality, she said, "In strategic asset management, we started with a premise that we needed to reorient the company to have an ROA mentality as opposed to strictly market share and P&L."

Again, the lever of change in breaking the P&L orientation of business-unit managers is the performance measurement system. Steve Newberry explained,

> What I did was create a greater sense of urgency here. I took the long-term objective for return on operating assets, which at one time was 36 percent, and I put it up at 44 percent. So our managers looked at that and said, "Heck, we're only at 25 percent now." My point to them is that they had better figure out what it is going to take. See, before they could get there at the peak of the cycle to 32 to 34 percent by pushing net income. You can't do that anymore. You can't get there without working the asset side of the equation.

If they are to be held accountable for the assets they employ, business-unit managers need to know which assets they own. Currently, Applied's financial systems cannot handle this requirement. For instance, significant chunks of the firm's research and demonstration labs are treated as shared (unassigned) assets by the product business units. Applied must decide if these labs will be owned by the corporation or the business units.

Finally, as senior management drives ownership of and accountability for assets down to the business units, they are taking steps to build business-unit management capability to carry out this responsibility. Newberry said,

> I think we still have a way to go to really educate the executives on how they can affect asset turnover. They do understand it intellectually, but market share and gross margin and what happens on that P&L side of the equation has been ingrained in them for so many years. So you evolve that over a couple years.... If we had a crisis, it would be different. We'd probably more aggressively do it.

With the focus having been on market share and margins for so long, change does not happen overnight. As Nancy Handel noted,

> These kinds of discipline take time to work their way through the company. I mean, I've been preaching asset management since 1992, and so here we are in 1997, and we just started to make reasonably substantive improvements in 1996. It just takes time. I'm willing to accept that if you come out with the best brand-new idea today, you're not going to get it implemented in the company tomorrow. Lean manufacturing is on its second year here, maybe its third year, and we're still trying to reorganize so that we can capture all the value....
>
> We teach asset management every time we get an invitation to try and encourage a new way of thinking and also to try and provide more [guidance about managing the asset base].

The strategic asset management initiative stands as an appropriate complement to the business process changes Applied is undertaking. The operational excellence and lean production initiatives represent management's effort to integrate business processes along the firm's value chain. The asset management initiative represents management's effort to decentralize the chain of command with regard to the ownership and accountability for assets. Together, these initiatives form the basis of Applied Materials' strategic transition. The jury is out on how successful Applied will be in achieving the ROA targets it has set for 2000. But nobody can fault management for being too narrow or cautious as it positions the company for another 20 years of profitable growth.

The Role of Applied's Financial Organization

As Applied has matured as a business organization, grown in size, and entered additional market segments, the model of management control it has employed over the past 20 years is evolving, and the role of finance is evolving as well. As business-unit managers become more financially literate and take on greater accountability for all financial aspects of their business units, the need for finance to focus on financial oversight lessens and the demand for decision support grows. The initiative by finance to share ownership of the balance-sheet review reflects this trend. According to Ed Brown, VP, Strategic Knowledge Solutions,

> As a company becomes more mature, the hygiene level develops, and basic kinds of finance work become institutionalized as part of everyone's job as opposed to being relegated to finance people—just like human resources and quality. How do you know that quality is in an organization? When you stop talking about it. It is already built into your job. So as people become more financially sound and can do their own forecasting, the role of finance changes. Finance used to be the ones that would say, "no," rather than ones that say, "yes but," or "here are the options," or whatever. I think that as the organization absorbs more of the hygiene level of finance, then finance staff can work closer and closer and be better business partners.

Driven by broader organizational changes and by its own vision, Applied's finance organization has been on a mission to change its role. In 1993, it initiated a formal process to define its vision and mission and a set of strategies to accomplish them. The strategies are three- to five-year initiatives that guide the establishment of annual objectives that also serve as the basis for finance staff bonuses. Financial executives refer to this process as "strategic alignment" of the financial organization with its internal customers.

The vision that resulted from this process is to "be a world-class strategic business partner providing a competitive advantage for Applied Materials." The key elements of this vision are a service orientation as business partner and a strategic focus on contributing to competitive advantage.

By its own assessment, the finance organization is too transaction driven. It is hampered by immature business processes, legacy systems, and skill sets that have too long emphasized traditional accounting and budgeting tasks. Too large a portion of its staff is deployed in these areas, leaving insufficient staff to service the decision support needs of the business units. Thus one of the financial organization's stated strategies is "to move from a transaction-driven to a strategic-driving organization." What we find most interesting is the seriousness and systematic way in which the financial organization is translating its commitment to be a business partner into the capabilities to perform as one. As Jerry Taylor explained,

> We want to move to a strategic guiding capability. The front-end interface of that is the product group controllers and the regional financial executives. But they've got to have better processes and better systems so we can rebalance the workload. And we've also got to invest in some strategic resources to help get us through that and then develop better ways of being sought out as a business partner.

As the financial organization makes its strategic transition, it is not about to disown its traditional fiduciary role. As the foregoing material has documented, the fiduciary role of the finance organization is a central element in Morgan's model of management control that is not open to debate. This model involves finance as a "strong functional home," with solid-line reporting by the business-unit controllers up through the CFO. Thus the financial organization's strategy is to extend its fiduciary role in such areas as business strategy, decision support, and issue management. Taylor noted,

> Everybody in the finance organization worldwide has a financial accountability into my office. And we believe that's crucial for ongoing operations…. Jim has always had this philosophy, which I endorse 100 percent, that in these fast-changing environments, you need stability in terms of accountability…. It's been very clear since the first day I came to work for Jim. He wants one person that he can look to on any single financial issue in the world. And it's my job if it isn't done right. It's very simple. He doesn't want it very confused.

> This thing works because I have the clout to say the buck stops here in terms of how we're going to account for this company. And we've done a good job of teaching that and then still trying to build as strong a business partnership arrangement as we can because we still have to do that to get operational support.

Service Orientation of the CFO Organization

This last comment by Taylor alludes to a key challenge in building the business partner role at Applied—managing the tension of a centrally run financial organization while making finance staff responsive members of their respective business-unit teams. A key mechanism that Taylor and his team have evolved to manage this tension is to tie finance staff bonuses to their success in satisfying their internal business customers.

In 1994, the finance organization instituted an improved process to align its efforts with its customers' needs. Financial managers interview their business customers to develop a list of critical needs. These needs are then incorporated into a formal set of management objectives and a performance scorecard. On a quarterly basis, line managers rate how well their respective financial organizations are meeting these objectives. Annually, these scorecard ratings exert a significant influence on finance staff bonus awards. As Taylor explained,

> Some of the stuff we've started is not worth much more than the paper it is on. Other stuff we've done pretty well. For example, as a finance organization we've moved from just talking about customer satisfaction to where we've put our bonuses on the line with feedback from management as to how well we are serving them on dedicated tasks where we said we would change something to be more supportive of management. I think that what we've done in that arena is probably pretty unique.

Mike O'Farrell elaborated on the customer satisfaction process:

> We try to quantify everything. We're not self-scoring. Others are scoring us. That's how our customer satisfaction process works. The firm has a process with the end customers who buy our products. And then we have a process internally, where a finance person will go to his business manager at the beginning of the year and ask, "What do you want from us this year?" They then set out the expectations given some practical constraints, because if someone doesn't know the cost of the effort, they may want everything. But they get down to what's important, they status during the year, the customer gives us a raw score from 1 to 10 and then signs the score sheet. It is their score, they sign it, and they remember signing it. This year we have seven major customer-satisfaction objectives. Each of those gets a customer scoring.

Steve Newberry commented on his satisfaction with this process and his desire to see it replicated by other staff organizations at Applied:

> Finance staff in a business unit are not tied to the incentive system that their business unit is. And that's key. If they are, you're going have the potential

that they might play with the numbers. So there's no motivation to do that. Now there's a problem with that. If those objectives are not aligned very well, then they might be off getting compensated for things the business units don't care about. So Jerry put a process in place back in the 1992–93 time frame. He's got a good partnering activity, where his staff develop, within the framework of the overall strategic objectives of finance, the specific focus that has to come in relative to each business unit.

If I asked the six or seven service groups that we have how many of them have a process by which they sit down each year and review each quarter what their common goals and objectives are for each group that they support, the answer is, finance is the only one. And how many of them have a customer satisfaction survey process that every quarter, customers fill out a customer satisfaction rating card against certain criteria and that is a major part of their executive incentive plan? The answer today is, only finance.

Strategic Focus of the CFO Organization

In addition to strengthening its service orientation, the financial organization's vision of business partner involves the development of its capability to influence business strategy. One example is the role it is playing under the leadership of Nancy Handel in the strategic asset management initiative. Many managers at Applied are supportive of greater involvement by finance in the strategic management of the firm.

Vinod Mahendroo, President of the Installed Base Support Services (IBSS) Business Product Group, views finance as an essential part of his management team. The IBSS business is to some degree the tail wagged by the product business groups' dog. Mahendroo must service and support the products installed by Applied's other business groups through customer engineers in the different regions. Also, the prices at which IBSS buys parts from suppliers who are selected by the system product business groups affect IBSS' profitability. Thus there are strong interdependencies between IBSS and the product groups and regions that must be managed. Mahendroo sees his finance organization as a key player in this process:

> If you think about a customer's fab[rication], they have to make a billion and a half dollars minimum bet with a two-year lead time without being able to predict the market. If they hit the market right, they recover the cost of the fab in the first seven months. If they hit it wrong, they never recover. It's such a high-risk business for them that whatever they can control, whatever they can leverage, they must. So they absolutely insist on a very high

level of support from us. Now think about the roles of finance in this environment. One, we need finance to be a very strong control function, with their fiduciary responsibility, and to protect the integrity of the IBSS P&L. Two, we need to have finance help with the connection with the rest of the company. So finance has to be a catalyst in the collaboration with the system product business groups and the regions. Three, we absolutely need finance to help us understand the business and understand the fundamentals, as the business deals with the fundamental strategy issues.

Tom St. Dennis also remarked about his expectations of his financial organization:

> Now, the finance group doesn't work for me. They are assigned to my organization. I would say that 95 percent of the time you can't tell a difference. I don't think that there is any question that they're aligned to these goals and objectives and that they're deployed on the teams that are helping us get this done. They have changed their financial systems to align to our product structures and our product plans... and I think the financial culture of Applied is unique among the companies that I've dealt with. It's very much a financial partner, a business partner—not a policeman. Not unbalanced in the decision process that they need to go through.

> What I love is that the finance organization talks our technology. They talk about our products. They talk about our competitors. They talk about our specific contribution to customer products.

Challenges of Change

On the whole, the business managers we talked with gave their finance staff high marks as business partners. But they also expressed some frustration that they did not have ample financial resources to manage their businesses. In some cases, they attributed this problem to the firm's legacy of centralized financial management. They felt that business-unit financial staff was too preoccupied with the needs of the corporate offices and, as a result, unable to adequately support the decision-making needs of the business unit. Julio Aranovich expressed it this way:

> If I go to my finance executive and I need to make a decision, it is substantive to me. It is absolutely unacceptable for that person to say, "I cannot because I need to do this report for the corporate office...." The fiduciary responsibility I would not dare to challenge. I agree. I support it. It is good that it exists. And my finance executive is the person to take care of that. Now I do not have to worry about that because somebody else is taking care of it. I can worry about the rest of the business. But my finance execu-

tive must also be the person on the executive staff who is in charge of our financial issues and business models.

In response to the lack of sufficient financial staff, Aranovich hired some additional finance people to supplement those allocated to him by the CFO organization. Other business units have done the same. He continued,

> We do not think that a shadow finance staff forever is a good thing. But we wanted to make a point in the hope of getting the corporation to change. Our point was that in every transaction there is a supplier and a customer. Bureaucracy is not the existence of an office, or of regulations and processes, or the existence of policies and law. Every single organization needs these. Bureaucracy is when any one of these departments is no longer in touch with its original objectives and itself becomes the objective. Bureaucracy is when finance forgets that their role is to help me make decisions and to run the business and when they believe their role is to be bigger, and more rich, and my agenda doesn't count. By the way, we all run the risk of becoming bureaucratic.

Apart from any preoccupation with corporate matters, the scarcity of financial resources has been aggravated by two major constraints: (1) Applied's immature business processes and legacy information systems require a tremendous amount of staffing that might otherwise be redeployed to higher value-added activities in the business units. (2) The CFO organization has had the objective of limiting its staff growth to half the growth rate of revenue. The intent here was to motivate finance staff to find ways to work smarter rather than just adding staff at the rate of the company's growth.

In recognition of the staffing problem raised by the business units, Jerry Taylor, the CFO, is relaxing this staffing constraint. Greg Miller talked about the first problem:

> You know what I have to do to cost products? Every single machine that ships out of Applied Materials is manually costed. We have ledgers that do the job 60 to 70 percent of the way, and then a finance person comes in and cleans up the mess and manually costs. So each of the 1,200 to 1,600 machines we ship each year is manually costed. Why do we have an army of cost accountants? It is because basically a cost accountant can handle about 40 machines.... You can do the math. And these machines are not only manually costed, they are manually forecasted. We suffer from constant complex configuration changes, poor engineering documentation and change control, and poor transaction processing discipline. These are some of the things we are trying to change.

In recognition of this problem, Applied's financial organization is participating in the business process improvements mentioned earlier in the case. Finance staff are also participating in a firm-wide initiative to install SAP, an enterprise information system. If things go as planned, the finance organization expects to free up a substantial percentage of its staff, which it will redeploy to new decision support initiatives in the areas of design-to-cost engineering, new product introduction and supply chain management, and activity analysis. Again, Miller spoke to this strategy:

> How do I measure success? I ask myself, have I redeployed a certain percentage of resources toward decision support, and are the initiatives farther along than they would have been without our support? Finance has a financial business process group which is dedicated to supporting all of the lean production initiatives. My staff and all of the divisional manufacturing finance staffs are in there supporting those initiatives. We're trying to make a difference. It's our vehicle to transform our work. A key part of our strategy is to change finance work and move our resources toward decision support.

The issue for Miller is not only headcount but also the skills that his staff will need to make the transition to higher value-added work, such as that just mentioned. He added,

> We are still very much a traditional accounting- and control-oriented organization. If you look at the composition of what our people spend their time on, they are principally consumed with closing the books, getting an accurate set of numbers, forecasting the business, actively engaging with the business to hit the short-term forecast, and casting a net of containment around poor business processes to avoid financial surprises.... So the kind of people we have working for us very much have the traditional controller and accounting skill set—because it's required to be successful here.

> As we transform our work, there are going to be casualties. I understand that some of the people who are doing the traditional accounting work may often be uncomfortable doing decision support.... It depends on the tools you are providing them and what you're asking them to do and how creative they have to be versus how well defined the work they do is.... Then there are other people who are absolutely just brilliant and just off and running.

Jerry Taylor discussed the challenges of transforming the finance organization even as the company has been growing at 53 percent a year:

> What you have to appreciate about a high-growth company, as we are, is that at all points in time no matter what your plan is, you have to live with

the fact that your capability is less than the opportunity. The issue is, how bad is the gap and are you making any progress in closing it.... But we've got to do more than just go work hard in this organization. And we've also got to have a strategy for how we add value over time. And then we've got a massive task to get all 600 to 700 people online simultaneously. That's a pretty big challenge.

But the vision is clear and the progress is unmistakable. The role of finance in fostering shared ownership of the balance-sheet review process and its involvement in the firm's strategic asset management initiative are evidence of this. The vision is clear, the initiatives to remove key obstacles are under way, and the commitment to business partnership and strategic contribution is shared by line managers and finance staff alike. As Greg Miller explained,

> Finance has a vision of what it wants to become. Essentially, we want to minimize or obsolete much of our current activities and become a business support group, a business advisor.

> That's a shared objective. That's an objective that Jerry wants, that's what finance wants. We call it value-added financial analysis. Ron Foster [Controller, Etch Group] has been calling it decision support. What we want to do is influence decisions. It all has to be pointed toward whether you get a better business decision, a better business result, because of finance.

> What will be different is that we will have effectively supported those business units that are trying to change the way they do business.... We will have effectively supported them, and they will be more successful than if finance hadn't.

Summing Up

In telling the Applied Materials story, we have described the management model that has contributed to the firm's outstanding track record of profitable growth and shareholder wealth creation over the past 20 years. No doubt, Applied's technological strength lies at the heart of its financial success. But it is the firm's management strength that we have focused on in this case.

Jim Morgan, Chairman and CEO, has followed a management model that has enabled Applied to maintain financial stability and profitability in the face of rapid technological change, high growth, and steep business cycles. The model counterbalances aggressive entrepreneurship in building technological capability and achieving market leadership with a highly disciplined system of financial management designed to avoid financial surprises and "contain the chaos" of Applied's high growth. The role of the CFO organization has been to champion the financial integrity of the forecasts that drive Applied's management review process and the financial reports made to its shareholders. The balance-sheet review process stands out as an exemplary practice in meeting these responsibilities.

Applied's senior management is repositioning the firm to cope with forces of industry maturation, globalization, and Applied's increased size. In a sense, Applied's management has recognized that success achieved by following a given management model ultimately renders that model obsolete. The model that carried the firm for the past 20 years is not necessarily the best one for the next 20.

Like Boeing, Applied Materials is evolving its management model in recognition of the maturation of its industry. Profitability is no longer solely related to bringing enabling chip-making technology first to market. Applied is making the transition to a balanced model of technological superiority and operational excellence. Applied's vision is that of "a big, fast, global competitor that is entrepreneurial and disciplined." Applied continues to expand the number of product markets it competes in, its share of market in each product segment, and its profitability.

While the fiduciary role remains paramount, the CFO organization is increasingly expected to support the decision-making and information needs of the decentralized business units. The role of finance staff as Business Advocates is assuming more and more importance. Under Jerry Taylor's leadership, the CFO organization has formulated a vision for itself as a world-class business partner. This vision has teeth. Finance staff bonuses are tied to achieving a set of concrete initiatives to the satisfaction of its internal customers. The CFO organization faces significant challenges in striking the proper balance between oversight and service to the business units, between independence and involvement in the business. The model of shared ownership that the finance organization is successfully implementing in the case of the balance-sheet review process and its involvement in and influence over the strategic asset management initiative suggest it is up to these challenges.

People Interviewed

Corporate Office

James Morgan
Chairman and CEO

Jerry Taylor
Senior Vice President and CFO

Stephen Newberry
Former Group Vice President, Global Operations and Planning

Edward Brown Jr.
Vice President, Strategic Knowledge Solutions

Seitaro Ishi
Vice President, Global Human Resources

Nancy Handel
Vice President, Corporate Finance, and Treasurer

Michael O'Farrell
Vice President and Corporate Controller

Business Units

Julio Aranovich
Vice President, Worldwide Manufacturing Operations

Vinod Mahendroo
President, Installed Base Support Services (IBSS)
Product Business Group

Tom St. Dennis
President, PVD Product Business Group

Paul Lindstrom
Vice President, Manufacturing

David Fried
Managing Director, CVD Product Business Group

Ron Foster
Controller, Etch Product Business Group

Gregory Miller
Controller, Worldwide Manufacturing Operations

7

Integration and Alignment

In the Introduction, we provided a brief summary of our previous research on the changing roles of financial management. Depending on the combination of the command-and-control, conformance, and competitive-team orientations to financial work, we found that financial people were either considered to be Business Advocates or Corporate Policemen. This new research study was designed to look at the financial management practices at firms that considered themselves to be, or are trying to become, Business Advocates.

As described in the Introduction, the Business Advocate model of financial management represents a combination of command-and-control and competitive-team orientations to financial work.

In a Business Advocate environment, financial people are expected to

  □   integrate business operations throughout the firm,

  □   think in terms of service and involvement,

  □   have a working knowledge of the business,

  □   encourage wide use of financial information, and

  □   provide financial discipline for the business operations.

Having worked our way through the individual firm case studies, we are in a position to summarize how the Business Advocate model is evolving in the five case-study firms. From our perspective, being or becoming a Business Advocate can be described with two words: integration and alignment.

If there is one overarching principle that characterizes the Business Advocate model of financial management, it would be *integration*.

Business Advocates are very adept at helping senior executives and line managers integrate business strategy, management control, and corporate accountability with their firm culture. We use the term "double integration" to refer to the two types of integration work that take place in our case-study firms. Business Advocates are either involved in

☐ integrating all of the firm's business operations through the financial organization, or

☐ integrating financial work into the fabric of the business through direct involvement in the business operations.

As documented in the individual case studies, financial people do not just become integrators. Senior management, in the person of the CEO, must want the CFO to create a Business Advocate financial organization. Given the mandate to build this type of financial organization, the CFO must focus on *alignment*.

The financial organization needs to be aligned with the business units and work together to achieve their common business objectives. As we found out, the alignment process has to be consistent with the current or changing corporate culture.

Integration

Although each of the firms included in this study uses some form of "balanced scorecard" to measure performance, only money measurement provides a basis for monitoring the performance of each of the firm's business operations as well as the financial performance of the entire firm. To a certain extent, managers working in the financial organization have a natural advantage over other managers in that they get to see how all the "parts" fit together to create the "whole" firm.

Given this natural advantage, financial people can go in one of two directions. They can develop their technical skills and become experts in a particular area of accounting or finance, or they can develop their interpersonal and communications skills and become managers who just happen to have a financial background. Most of the financial people we interviewed at the five case-study firms had followed the managerial track.

Managers with a strong financial background are expected to

☐ build financial discipline into business operations,

☐ get involved in the design and development of performance measurement and incentive compensation systems, and

☐ help develop the financial competency of operating managers and employees.

The second type of integration requires financial people to "share" control and become "partners" with operating managers. In this type of integration, financial information is shared among all members of the business-unit team, and people with financial backgrounds have management responsibilities that extend beyond pure accounting and finance.

Each of the five aspects of the "double integration" theme will be illustrated by reference to the material contained in the individual case studies.

Build Financial Discipline into Business Operations

Caterpillar

In a highly centralized, bureaucratic organization, financial discipline is imposed on the functional units and departments through the budget. Financial discipline exercised in this manner means living within your budget and spending all of your money before year-end. The firm could be in serious financial trouble, but as long as managers lived within their budgets, they received a positive evaluation.

The reorganization that took place in the early 1990s was designed to rectify that situation. In the new decentralized organization, success was defined in terms of meeting the business-unit objectives. "Accountable profit" and "accountable assets" provided the new basis for maintaining financial discipline. Under the new organization, managers were given full responsibility for their own income statements and balance sheets. Instead of financial discipline being imposed from corporate headquarters, the business units had to develop their own capability for maintaining financial discipline. As discussed more fully below, that responsibility fell on the business manager, typically a person who came up through the ranks of the financial organization.

Applied Materials

Historically, financial discipline at Applied Materials has been split between the business units and the corporate financial organization. The business units "owned" the income statement and were held accountable for market shares, revenues, expenses, and operating profit. On behalf of corporate executive management, the corporate financial organization owned the balance sheet and monitored the investment in receivables, inventory, and facilities.

Financial discipline was maintained by the corporate financial group through the balance-sheet review process. The purpose of the balance-sheet review is to highlight business risks and make sure these risks are accounted for by establishing the appropriate reserves for inventories and receivables and establishing accrued liabilities for product warranties. Applied's balance-sheet review process epitomizes the disciplined character of Applied's approach to management control. The review process has been designed to avoid financial surprises.

In recent years, Applied's financial organization has taken the initiative to shift ownership of the balance-sheet review to the business units. In the past, the business-unit controller was responsible for the balance-sheet review. Today, the business-unit manager is responsible for conducting the review with the support of the business-unit controller.

BellSouth

BellSouth represents a third example of providing financial discipline for the business operations. The corporate CFO is using the budget-planning and resource-allocation process as the vehicle for transforming BellSouth from a company with a regulated monopoly mindset to a company with a competitive market mindset. DCF analysis underlies BellSouth's approach to financial discipline.

Nucor

Nucor represents the ultimate example of financial discipline being completely integrated into the fabric of the business. Nucor's incentive compensation system covers all employees and is tied directly to the performance of all employees covered by one of the four compensation plans. By virtue of the design of this compensation system, Nucor has no need for a separate cadre of financial staff to maintain a separate financial measurement system to monitor performance.

The Nucor story is instructive in the sense that line managers and front-line workers have internalized their own financial discipline. As illustrated by the financial management practices at Nucor, a firm does not need a lot financial people to maintain financial discipline. Financial discipline at Nucor is just one component of how "lean administration" works in a high-trust environment.

Get Involved in Design and Development

One way to give financial people the opportunity to develop their integration skills is by having the CFO organization centrally involved in the design and development of key change or improvement initiatives. At four of the five case-study firms, major initiatives are under way that involve financial people. The individual case studies detail the specifics of these initiatives. At one firm, the change initiated in the mid-1960s proved so successful that most of the efforts since that time have been focused on fine-tuning the system.

Nucor

Nucor is the one firm in our study that has not undertaken any major transformation initiatives in the recent past. The reason is quite simple. The current business model put into place by Ken Iverson and Sam Siegel when they took over management of the company has served Nucor so well that it does not need to be changed. To a large extent, the change initiatives occurring at the other case-study firms are moving those firms closer to the Nucor model.

Caterpillar

In 1990, Caterpillar undertook the major reorganization that transformed it from a highly centralized, functional organization into a decentralized, customer-focused organization. As part of its contribution to the success of the reorganization, the corporate accounting group designed, developed, and implemented the measurement system to be used in the new decentralized organization. That assignment included the design and development of the market-based transfer pricing system that underlies Caterpillar's entire system of corporate accountability.

Since that time, the corporate accounting group has designed and developed a series of innovative business education games to help business-unit personnel understand and adapt to the new business organization.

Applied Materials

The CFO organization is involved in the design and development of Applied's strategic asset management initiative, which seeks to significantly improve the company's return on operating assets. This initiative will require the corporate financial organization to move away from a transactions-processing mode of operations to a strategy-based mode of operations.

Boeing

The CFO organization was the architect of the firm's new employee stock-ownership program. The finance organization developed this program in direct response to the CEO's desire that all employees share in the financial success of the company. As Boeing engages its employees by sharing the value created on behalf of the shareholders, management is attempting to push responsibility for managing the economics of the business down to the shop floor.

BellSouth

The CFO organization is leading the way in transforming the company from a regulated monopoly to a market competitor. The CFO organization is leading the charge to transform BellSouth from a rate-of-return-driven company to a market-driven company, where "market" refers to both customer markets and capital markets. Now that guaranteed returns are a thing of the past, BellSouth must move from capital-based planning to market-based planning.

Help Develop Financial Competency

The CEOs at Caterpillar and Boeing have made a commitment to increasing the business competency of senior executives, line managers, and employees. At first glance, most of us would assume that senior managers possess the appropriate amount of business competency, otherwise they would not be senior executives. However, if we remember that many of these managers worked their way up through a particular functional specialty, we can more easily see the need for more training and development. In many cases, the knowledge they possess is deep (in their functional area of expertise) but not wide (in a general management sense).

Based on our interviews at these two firms, increasing business competency is a priority in the financial area. In both firms, the CFO organization has been charged with helping managers and employees become more financially literate.

Caterpillar

Caterpillar's corporate accounting group has developed a series of financial games designed to develop specific business competencies. The accountability game was developed to help managers, engineers, and plant workers understand such concepts as ROA, market-based transfer pricing, and accountable profit that underlie the measurement system used to evaluate the performance of the 17 profit center divisions and 5 service center divisions.

The accountability game was so successful that the financial organization developed three other games to improve business competency: the cash flow game, the currency game, and the cost connection. The cash flow game provides students with the opportunity to learn how Caterpillar uses cash flow and DCF analysis for sourcing studies, product planning, and capital budgeting.

Since Caterpillar manufactures and sources worldwide, product managers and engineers must also understand the dynamics of and risks associated with foreign currency exchange. The currency game was designed to meet this need. Finally, the newest kid on the block is the cost connection. The corporate accounting group developed the cost connection to help product planners and engineers understand the relationship between product costs and the profit for which business-unit managers are held accountable.

Boeing

The source of Boeing's competitive advantage and the core of CEO Phil Condit's vision of people working together is a committed and competent workforce. The recently established employee stock-ownership program represents a significant step toward building workforce commitment. As part of his notion that Boeing's workforce must become less discipline focused and more business focused, Condit has established a firmwide initiative to develop the business competencies of its managers, engineers, production workers, and sales force.

The CFO organization has been charged with the responsibility of increasing business competency in finance—the language of value, DCF, and cost flow. Boeing's finance staff has begun the education process by developing instructional materials on shareholder value and DCF for the senior manager group. Efforts are now under way to extend that training to the next level of management.

Integrate Operating and Financial Systems

Once the workforce is educated about how to run a business, managers and other employees expect to have access to the financial information they need to run their part of the business. Put another way, it is not possible to integrate financial work into the fabric of the business if workers do not have access to financial information. Once you start down the road with an operating philosophy that emphasizes people working together with a shared stake in the business, the need to share financial information becomes obvious. If workers and managers are expected to act like owners, they must have access to the information that owners use to evaluate the success of the business. This information-sharing philosophy is present to some degree in all of the case studies.

Nucor

Nucor has the most open information philosophy of all five case-study firms. Executives trace this philosophy back to former President Dave Aycock, whose belief was, "You either tell your workforce everything or tell them nothing. If you try and do it halfway in between, then people worry about what you are not telling them." So management lets employees see all of the financial information about their division and the other divisions throughout Nucor.

Caterpillar

If managers at Caterpillar are to be held accountable for their profits and their assets, they need to monitor their performance on a timely basis. They also need to know that they approved every dollar of expense and capital that appears on their financial statements. Within the business units, every member of the management team has access to their financial information.

Boeing

Boeing is just beginning to tackle the issue of open-book management. As part of a business competency leadership team, the CFO organization is developing a model of open-book management that reflects the connection between ownership, business competence, and openness.

Expand Management Responsibilities

At each of the case-study firms, we interviewed individuals who were considered to be financial managers but whose responsibilities extended well beyond accounting and finance. They had financial backgrounds but were really business managers. As business managers, they had cross-functional responsibilities: accounting and reporting, financial planning and control, HR, procurement, information technology, contracts, scheduling, and labor relations.

Because most of the day-to-day accounting and other support functions have been computerized, fewer people are needed to carry out these functions. A single person can now manage and coordinate the human aspects of these support services. In our case-study firms, those business managers have typically come up through the financial organization instead of from other administrative support service groups.

Caterpillar
At Caterpillar, business-unit controllers are now called "business managers" in recognition of their broader responsibilities and partnership role.

Boeing
This past year, Boeing has instituted the title of Vice President of Business Resources for the Defense and Space Group and the Boeing Commercial Aircraft Group. These positions have been filled by managers from the financial organization.

Nucor
Nucor still uses the term "plant controller," but each controller functions as assistant general manager for the plant. The individuals who perform the accounting and reporting functions report to the plant controller along with individuals heading the other administrative support services. Virtually all of the plant controllers are CPAs with some public accounting experience.

Applied Materials
By CEO edict, the CFO organization is independent of line operations. All finance staff report directly to the CFO. Given Finance's independent status, financial people are "recruited out" of the financial organization to fill business manager positions in the business units.

At all five case-study firms, many individuals with financial backgrounds are faced with the choice of remaining technical specialists or becoming managers. At Caterpillar and Nucor, individuals can choose to become managers and remain in the financial organization. At Boeing and Applied Materials, becoming a business manager means leaving the financial organization.

Alignment

The integration of financial work into the fabric of the business is fostered when the interests and goals of the financial organization are aligned with those of the business units. Alignment is fostered through shared ideals and incentives. First and foremost, alignment between finance and the rest of the organization is enhanced when the role of the finance organization is couched in terms of service and involvement as opposed to oversight and surveillance. Service and involvement are cornerstones of the Business Advocate financial organization.

Caterpillar
At Caterpillar, the internal market for financial services is used to align the financial organization with the business units. In using a market mechanism to align the financial organization (and other support services) with the business units, Caterpillar has instilled a customer focus throughout the entire firm.

In Caterpillar's decentralized organization, there are 17 profit center divisions and 5 support service divisions (which were the old general office functions). As a support service group, corporate accounting has to recover all of its costs by selling its services to the profit center divisions. If corporate accounting cannot convince its customers to buy its services, it will have a "cost problem" that has to be eliminated by cutting costs and reducing headcount.

Corporate accounting has converted a potential cost problem into a service opportunity. For instance, corporate accounting has created an internal consulting group that rivals its public accounting counterparts.

Nucor
All members of Nucor's workforce participate in one of four incentive compensation programs. The interests of the members of the financial organization are aligned with the interests of their respective business units and/or corporate headquarters.

The incentive compensation for the financial people within the divisions is based on the same ROA calculation for all other staff personnel in their divisions. The incentive compensation for the CFO and corporate controller is based on the same ROE calculation for all other executives at corporate headquarters.

Applied Materials

By CEO edict, the CFO organization is independent of the business units. Given this independent status, the question arises as to how the CFO organization can align its interests with those of its business-unit customers.

Applied's solution to this quandary has been to tie finance staff incentive compensation to the formal satisfaction ratings it receives from its internal customers.

Conclusion

As we have seen from the discussion in this chapter, the Business Advocate model of financial management plays out somewhat differently in each of the case-study firms. Looking at all five firms as a group, we see that the common themes are integration and alignment.

The financial organization cannot function as a Business Advocate unless the CEO sees the benefits of service and involvement rather than oversight and surveillance. However, once that decision has been made, the CFO has to develop a strategy for aligning the financial organization with the business units. Once aligned with the business units, financial people can be called upon to be "double integrators." As Business Advocates, financial people can get involved in integrating all of the firm's business operations through the financial organization and integrating financial work into the fabric of the business through direct involvement in the business operations.

Appendix

Interview Protocols

For Corporate-Level Executives

During this interview, we would like to develop a basic understanding of how you see business strategy, management controls, and shareholder accountability being integrated within your firm. We are particularly interested in your perceptions of the role the financial organization plays and the capabilities it brings to the strategy, control, and accountability process.

1. Please describe the career path you have followed to reach your present position, and how your experiences have influenced the way you think about your current responsibilities.

2. What are two or three most significant personal or organizational challenges currently facing you as a member of the senior management team? How do you translate these challenges into goals and objectives you set for your organization? What initiatives have you undertaken to achieve these goals?

3. What role do senior financial executives or other members of the financial organization play in the formulation and implementation of business strategy? What role does the financial organization play in helping the businesses create shareholder value?

4. As part of the overall management control process, have significant changes been made in the way the financial organization contributes to the overall success of the firm? In what areas does the financial organization still need to change in order to make the overall business more successful?

5. Of the major corporate initiatives that have been undertaken over the past several years, how many have involved the cooperative effort of financial and nonfinancial managers? Have any

of these joint ventures made a significant difference in how business is conducted within your firm?

6. To what extent have efforts to improve the effectiveness of the financial organization come from senior management outside the financial organization, or have efforts to improve effectiveness come from within the financial organization?

For Operating-Level Financial and Nonfinancial Managers

During this interview, we would like to develop a basic understanding of how you see business strategy, management controls, and shareholder accountability being integrated within your firm. We are particularly interested in your perceptions of the role the financial organization plays and the capabilities it brings to the strategy, control, and accountability process.

The following questions are couched in the context of a specific initiative in which you are involved to improve the business strategy, control, and accountability process.

1. Who initiated this particular functional or cross-functional project?

2. What was the main objective in initiating the project?

3. How many people were involved in the change process? What were their titles and functional responsibilities before joining the team?

4. What personal benefits did you derive from being a member of this team? What were the greatest frustrations?

5. When we talk to your colleagues at the next level above or below you in the organization, what are they likely to identify as the greatest benefits to be derived from this project? What costs are they likely to say they have incurred as a result of the project?

6. Did this particular project draw the business or functional units closer together or drive them farther apart? Did the project result

in significant headcount reductions, resource reallocations, or changes in authority and responsibility?

7. If we were to reinterview you two years from now, how would you evaluate the success or failure of this particular project?

About the Authors

Dr. Stephen F. Jablonsky is a faculty member at The Pennsylvania State University and senior member of The Management Communications Group.

As a faculty leader in executive education programs, Dr. Jablonsky helps managers see how they can develop a better understanding of their business through financial information. In programs tailored to meet the needs of specific clients, the main focus is on improving the financially based communication skills of cross-functional management teams. His new book, *The Manager's Guide to Financial Statement Analysis* (John Wiley, 1998), presents the financial concepts and tools that underlie his approach to increasing the effectiveness of financially based management communications.

As a researcher and consultant, Dr. Jablonsky is interested in how firms integrate business strategy, management control, and corporate accountability within their overall culture. The Management Communications Group maintains a database of over 3,000 responses to the current version of the diagnostic questionnaire (DQ5) introduced in *Business Advocate or Corporate Policeman? Assessing Your Role as a Financial Executive* (FERF 1993). DQ5 provides the basis for helping clients assess their own management operating philosophies.

Dr. Jablonsky has written articles for *Strategic Management Journal, Academy of Management Review, Financial Executive, Organizational Behavior and Human Performance, Socio-Economic Planning Sciences,* and *Management Accounting,* among others.

Dr. Jablonsky received his BS (1967), MAS (1968), and PhD (1974) in accountancy at the University of Illinois. He received a CPA in Illinois in 1966.

Dr. Patrick J. Keating is Professor of Business Administration in the Department of Accounting and Finance at San Jose State University. Dr. Keating's primary research interest lies in understanding the determinants of effective financial management.

Dr. Keating has published articles in *Financial Executive, Management Accounting*, and the *Journal of Management Accounting Research*. He has presented on such topics as "The New Role of the CFO: Financial Management for the Lean Enterprise," to members of the Mexican Financial Executives Institute in Puerto Vallarta, Mexico; "The Role of Finance in Target Costing," to members of Computer Aided Manufacturing International (CAM-I); and "The Changing Role of Finance in American Companies: Core Values and Capabilities," to Japanese financial executives in Tokyo, Japan.

Dr. Keating received a PhD in business administration from The Pennsylvania State University, where he also earned an undergraduate degree in electrical engineering, and received a master's degree in public policy from the University of Michigan. In addition to his years of teaching and research, Dr. Keating's professional background includes financial administration and information systems development.

Drs. Jablonsky and Keating are the coauthors of *Changing Roles of Financial Management: Getting Close to the Business* (FERF 1990), and with James B. Heian, of *Business Advocate or Corporate Policeman? Assessing Your Role as a Financial Executive* (FERF 1993).

Acknowledgments

Over the past ten years, the Financial Executives Research Foundation, Inc. (FERF™) has provided us with the opportunity to study the changing roles of financial management in major U.S. corporations. We have had the opportunity to interview senior corporate executives and financial and nonfinancial managers at all levels throughout our case-study firms. In particular, we wish to thank Bob Moore, Roland Laing, Jim Lewis, and Bill Sinnett for encouraging and supporting our research efforts. We are also deeply indebted to Boyd A. Givan, Senior Vice President and CFO at Boeing and former Chairman of FERF. Without his personal support, we might never have had the opportunity to extend our original *Changing Roles* research. We are indebted as well to our contact persons at each of the participating firms for their role in making our company visits so enjoyable and successful. Without the efforts of Lou Jones of Caterpillar, Sam Siegel at Nucor, Ron Dykes of BellSouth, Curt Nohavec of Boeing, and Mike O'Farrell of Applied Materials, we could not have completed this research project.